THE SCIENCE
FACTORY

JON RICHARDS

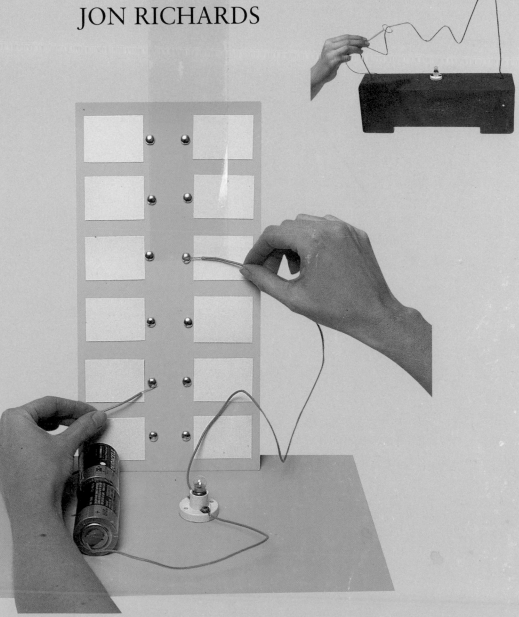

COPPER BEECH BOOKS
BROOKFIELD, CONNECTICUT

© Aladdin Books Ltd 2000

Designed and produced by
Aladdin Books Ltd
28 Percy Street
London W1P 0LD

ISBN 0-7613-0832-6

First published in the United States
in 2000 by
Copper Beech Books,
an imprint of
The Millbrook Press
2 Old New Milford Road
Brookfield, Connecticut 06804

Editors
Kathy Gemmell
Michael Flaherty

Design
David West
Children's Book Design

Designers
Jennifer Skelly
Flick Killerby

Cover Design
Sofie Hellemans

Illustrators
Ian Moores, Ian Thompson

Printed in The U.A.E.

Some of the illustrations in this book
have appeared in previous titles
published by Aladdin Books.

All the photos in this book were
taken by Roger Vlitos.

Cataloging-in-Publication Data is on
file at the Library of Congress.

5 4 3 2 1

INTRODUCTION

Have you ever thought how sounds are made, how light travels, how magnets work, or what life would be like without electricity? Do you know how boats float, how submarines sink, or how airplanes fly?

For many years scientists have experimented with air, water, light, sound, magnetism, machines, measuring, chemicals, structures, and electricity – now you can do the same.

The Science Factory has carefully planned step-by-step projects for you to try. A "Why It Works" panel explains the science behind each project and further ideas provide extra fun and more information. It's the best way to learn about science!

CONTENTS

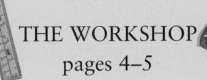

THE WORKSHOP

BEFORE YOU START any of the projects, it is important that you learn a few simple rules about the care of your science factory.

● Always keep your hands and the work surfaces clean. Dirt can damage results and ruin a project.

● Read the instructions carefully before you start each project.

● Make sure you have all the equipment you need for the project (see checklist opposite).

● If you haven't got the right piece of equipment, then improvise. For example, any paper that you can see through will do just as well as tracing paper.

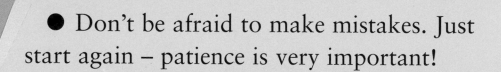

● Don't be afraid to make mistakes. Just start again – patience is very important!

WARNING:
Some of the projects in this book need the help of an adult. Always ask a grown-up to give you a hand with sharp objects such as scissors, or electrical appliances.

Equipment checklist:

- Scissors, tape (adhesive and double sided), and glue
- Plastic bottles and fruit-juice cartons
- Oil-based paints, paintbrush, powder paints, and turpentine
- Potato, salt, flour, red cabbage, butter, sugar, and lemon
- Vinegar, milk, and food coloring
- Colored paper and colored cardboard (thin and thick), white paper and cardboard
- Newspaper and tissue paper
- Modeling clay, candles, and sponges
- Large glass bowl and drinking glasses
- Jars (some with cork lid) and measuring cup
- Aluminum foil and colored cellophane
- Paper clips, brass paper fasteners, bulldog clips, stapler, and pins
- Insulated, bare, and stiff wire
- Drinking straws and balloons
- Plastic cups and beakers
- Metal waste basket and glass bottles
- Toothpicks, sticks, and used matchsticks
- Cotton thread, colored wool, and cotton balls
- Sprout seeds and wool cloth
- Dust cloths and old towels
- Yarn and dish towel
- Rubber bands, plastic wrap, and plastic bag
- Bottle caps, metal lid, and thumbtacks
- Empty spools and string
- Cardboard tubes and lid
- Ticking clock, alarm clock, and watch
- Ping-Pong ball, toy cars
- Bowls, ice-cube tray, and egg cartons
- Foil trays and empty spray can
- Wooden disk, hair dryer, pipe cleaners, and baking tray.
- Blindfold

- Weight and ribbons
- Large cardboard boxes
- Thin foil candy wrappers
- 3 volt and 6 volt lightbulbs and sockets
- Adhesive vinyl
- Styrofoam blocks and boards
- Wire coat hanger
- Plastic lids and pencil lead
- Blotting, filter, and tracing paper
- Books, marbles
- Flashlights and rulers
- Permanent and water-based felt-tip pens
- Small mirrors and blankets
- Eyepiece and convex lenses
- Glass jars
- Magnets of several shapes
- Magnetic and nonmagnetic objects
- Flowerpot tray and shallow dish
- Sand and iron filings
- Batteries (1.5 V)
- Copper coins
- Compasses
- Needles (steel), iron nails, and corks
- Pencil and pen
- Paper plates
- Pitcher of water
- Protractor
- Sheet of plastic film
- Small container
- Small objects, wooden blocks, pole, wooden dowels, and piece of wood
- Thick boards
- Corkboard and 2 large boards
- Cooking fat, yeast, and baking powder
- Plaster of Paris and model trees
- Soil, saw, sieve, and small candle
- Kitchen knife, saucepan, and long spoon
- Washing soda, skewer, and splint
- Colored pencils
- Plastic tray

CHAPTER 1

AIR & FLIGHT

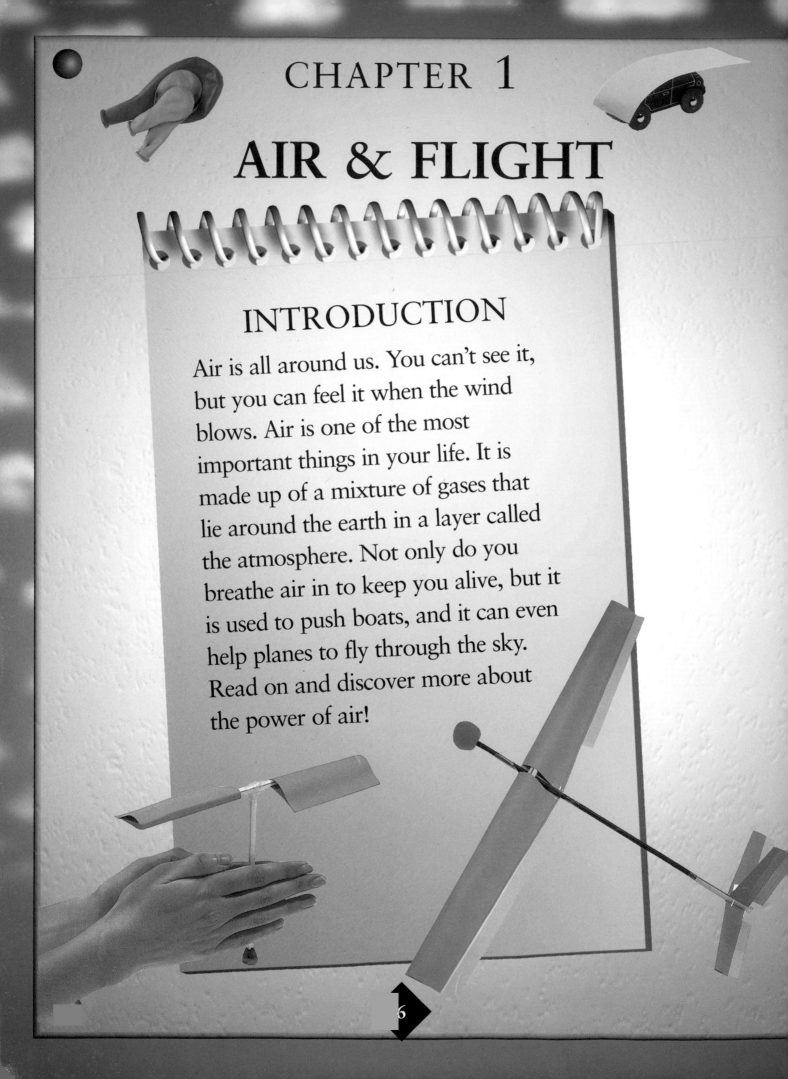

INTRODUCTION

Air is all around us. You can't see it, but you can feel it when the wind blows. Air is one of the most important things in your life. It is made up of a mixture of gases that lie around the earth in a layer called the atmosphere. Not only do you breathe air in to keep you alive, but it is used to push boats, and it can even help planes to fly through the sky. Read on and discover more about the power of air!

CONTENTS

GOING UP

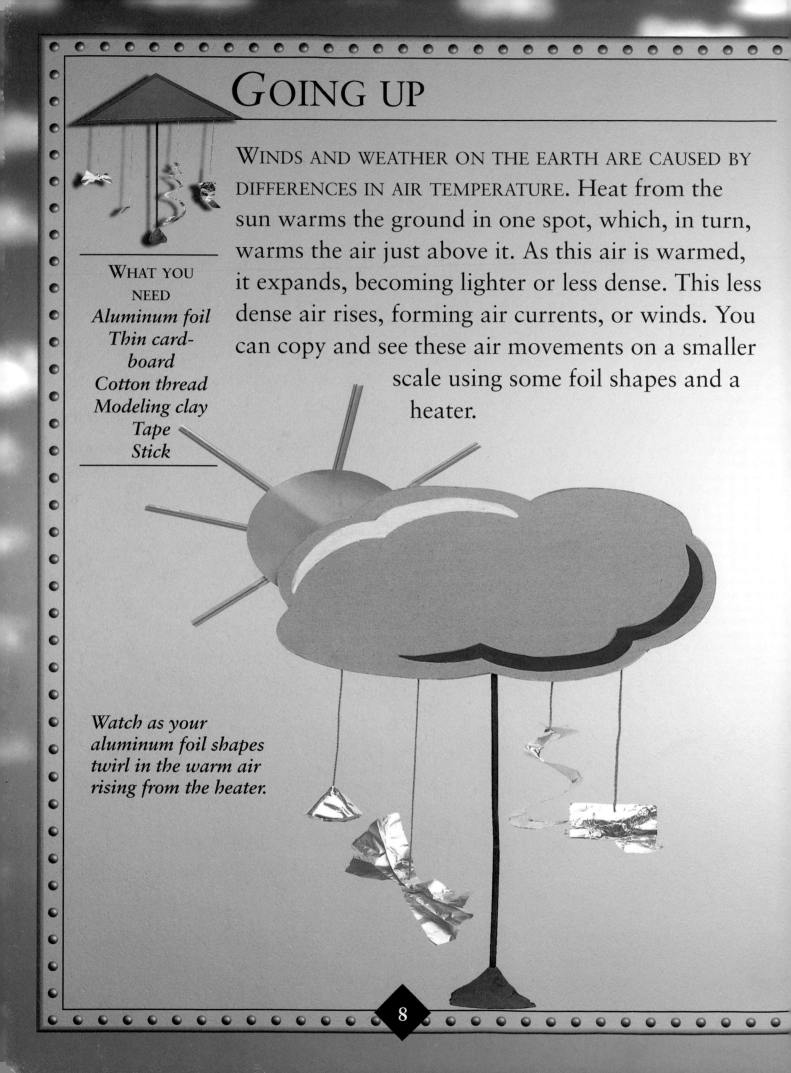

Aluminum foil
Thin card-board
Cotton thread
Modeling clay
Tape
Stick

WINDS AND WEATHER ON THE EARTH ARE CAUSED BY DIFFERENCES IN AIR TEMPERATURE. Heat from the sun warms the ground in one spot, which, in turn, warms the air just above it. As this air is warmed, it expands, becoming lighter or less dense. This less dense air rises, forming air currents, or winds. You can copy and see these air movements on a smaller scale using some foil shapes and a heater.

Watch as your aluminum foil shapes twirl in the warm air rising from the heater.

MOBILE AIR

1 *Cut some strips of aluminum foil into shapes.*

2 *Attach a length of cotton thread to each foil shape.*

3 *Cut a large cloud shape out of cardboard, fix it to a stick, and secure a piece of modeling clay to the base. Make sure that it will stand up.*

4 *Attach the foil shapes to the cardboard cloud and place your mobile above a heater — keep it away from any flames.*

WHY IT WORKS

Air above the heater is warmed, becomes less dense, and starts to rise. This rising warm air pushes against your foil shapes, causing them to turn.

DIRECTION OF MOVEMENT

ALUMINUM SHAPES DEFLECTED BY WARM AIR

ALUMINUM SHAPES

RISING WARM AIR

ALL SHAPES AND SIZES

See how well some other foil shapes spin. You will find that some shapes spin better because they are deflected more easily by the rising warm air.

TWISTED LOOP   CURVE

HOT-AIR BALLOON

BECAUSE HOT AIR RISES (SEE PAGES 8–9), it can be used to lift things into the air. For more than 200 years, people have flown through the air in hot-air balloons. The first hot-air balloon was built in 1783 by two French brothers, Joseph and Jacques Montgolfier. This experiment shows how to build your own miniature hot-air balloon and how it can fly.

WHAT YOU NEED
Tissue paper
Glue
Cardboard
Cotton thread
Hair dryer

UP, UP, AND AWAY

1 Fold a sheet of tissue paper in half and cut out one panel for your hot-air balloon.

2 Repeat this using different colors of tissue paper, until you have cut out four panels.

3 Glue the edges of your panels together to make your balloon.

4 Fold a piece of cardboard to make a small basket and attach it to the bottom of your balloon using four lengths of cotton thread.

WHY IT WORKS

The air inside your balloon is warmer and less dense than the air outside it. As a result, this air inside the balloon rises, carrying the balloon up with it.

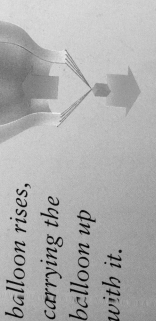

WARM AIR INSIDE THE BALLOON

5 Blow the balloon up with hot air from a hair dryer. Watch it rise from the ground.

GETTING HEAVY

Make some figures out of modeling clay and place them inside the balloon's basket. You will find that the more weight the balloon has to carry, the harder it will be to fly.

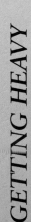

Sailing away

FOR THOUSANDS OF YEARS, sailors have been using the wind to push their boats along. Although engines and propellers are more widely used today, some boats, from small yachts to larger cruise liners, are still fitted with wind-catching sails. Make your own yacht and see how a sail catches the wind.

Float your boat in a bathtub full of water. Turn the sail so that it has its back to you while the boat points in another direction. Blow hard on the sail and watch the boat travel in the direction that the boat is pointing.

SAIL POWER

1 Cut a rectangular piece out of the side of a plastic bottle to make your boat's body.

2 Fix a lump of modeling clay in the bottom of your boat and use it to hold a straw mast.

3 Cut a triangular piece of paper to make a sail and pierce two holes in it to thread your mast through.

4 Cut out a wedge-shaped piece from a fruit-juice carton — this will be your keel. Fix a lump of model-ing clay to each end and stick the keel to the boat's bottom.

WHY IT WORKS

As the wind catches the sail it tries to push the boat sideways. However, the resistance of the water on the keel stops the boat from going sideways. Instead the boat is pushed forward.

DIRECTION OF BOAT'S TRAVEL

SAIL

DIRECTION OF WIND

KEEL

WATER RESISTANCE

MOVING YOUR SAILS

Try moving the position of your sail. You will find that the boat moves with less control when the sail is not above the keel.

SAIL FIXED AT FRONT

SAIL FIXED AT REAR

TELLING THE WEATHER

WHAT YOU NEED
Glass jar
Thin cardboard
Drinking straw
Toothpick
Tape, Balloon
Rubber band

EVEN THOUGH YOU CAN'T SEE IT, air has weight. The tiny molecules that make up air are attracted to the earth by gravity, making them press on you. This is called air pressure. Air pressure is changing all the time, as air currents move over the planet and the weather changes. You can make a device that measures these changes in air pressure — it's called a barometer.

RAIN OR SHINE?

1 Cut the neck off a balloon and stretch the balloon over a glass jar. Secure the balloon with a rubber band.

2 Tape a toothpick to the end of a straw and tape the other end of the straw to the center of the balloon lid.

3 Fold a sheet of cardboard and fix a cardboard triangle to the back to support it. Fix a pressure chart in place showing good weather at the top and bad weather at the bottom.

FEEL THE PRESSURE

Try to lever up some paper using a ruler. Air pressure on the paper will make this quite hard. You can see the weight of air by balancing two full balloons, then emptying one.

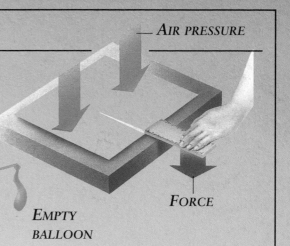

AIR PRESSURE

FORCE

FULL BALLOON

EMPTY BALLOON

4 Put the barometer in front of the chart and mark where the pointer moves up and down over a few days.

WHY IT WORKS

Changes in air pressure will cause the balloon lid to bend, moving the pointer. A rise in air pressure is a sign of good weather, and a fall in air pressure is a sign of bad weather.

HIGHER AIR PRESSURE PUSHES DOWN ON THE BALLOON

POINTER RISES

POINTER FALLS

LOWER AIR PRESSURE CAUSES THE BALLOON TO BEND OUT

FALLING PRESSURE

HAVE YOU NOTICED HOW FAST-MOVING OBJECTS, such as cars and trains, seem to pull objects after them when they race by? This is because these fast objects push air along quickly. As the objects push air along, they create low pressure behind them, and air from around the sides is sucked in to equal out the difference in pressure. You can see this effect in action with this phenomenon.

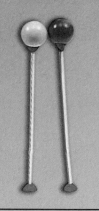

WHAT YOU NEED

Two Ping-Pong balls
Two straws
Modeling clay
Hair dryer

BLOWING BALLS

1 *Stick small lumps of modeling clay to the ends of two drinking straws. The best straws to use are the flexible type with the crinkled section.*

2 *Attach Ping-Pong balls onto the modeling clay at the ends of the straws farthest from the crinkled section. Stick the other ends of the straws onto a flat surface, making sure that the straws can stand up.*

AIR SQUEEZE

Blow between two sheets of paper. The low air pressure created by your blowing causes the sheets to come together.

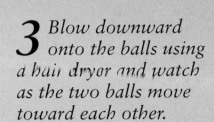

3 Blow downward onto the balls using a hair dryer and watch as the two balls move toward each other.

WHY IT WORKS

The fast-moving air flowing between the two balls creates an area of low pressure between the balls. The balls are then pushed together by higher air pressure outside them.

FAST-MOVING AIR

HIGHER PRESSURE

BALLS MOVE TOGETHER

LOWER AIR PRESSURE BETWEEN BALLS

RISING PAPER

Blow over the surface of a piece of paper held by your mouth. The air you blow out creates an area of low air pressure above the paper, which causes the paper to rise.

SHARP SHAPE

WHAT YOU NEED
Two identical toy cars
Thin cardboard
Tape
Hair dryer

HAVE YOU NOTICED THAT FAST RACING CARS ARE VERY POINTED? This streamlined shape lets them move through the air more easily and quickly. On the other hand, objects with an unstreamlined shape can be slowed down as they travel through the air. These experiments will show you how an object's shape can affect its movement.

The car covered by the curved cardboard will experience less air resistance and will travel down the ramp faster than the other car.

SLOWING THE FALL

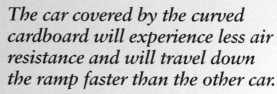

Make a parachute by tying some cotton thread to four corners of a handkerchief. Fix a lump of modeling clay to the other ends of the cotton thread and throw it in the air. The parachute slows its fall because it traps air molecules under it, creating air resistance.

WHY IT WORKS

The car with the curved cardboard travels faster because its shape disturbs the air less. The car with the unstreamlined body disturbs the air. This disturbed air increases the force called drag, which slows the car down.

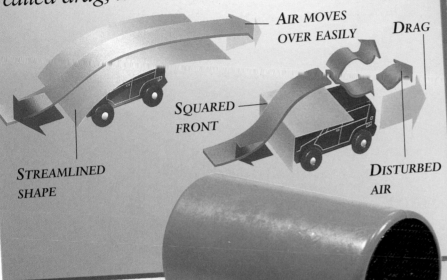

AIR MOVES
OVER EASILY

DRAG

SQUARED
FRONT

STREAMLINED
SHAPE

DISTURBED
AIR

STREAMLINED SHAPES

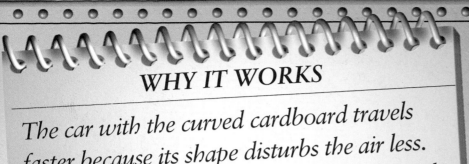

1 Take two identical model cars. Make sure that each moves as easily as the other. Cut out cardboard rectangles that will cover the cars.

2 Attach the rectangles to the front of the cars. Fold one smoothly over the top to form a curve and bend the other one to form a right angle.

3 Tilt a board on a book to form a ramp. Release the cars from the top of the ramp at the same time into a wind caused by the hair dryer.

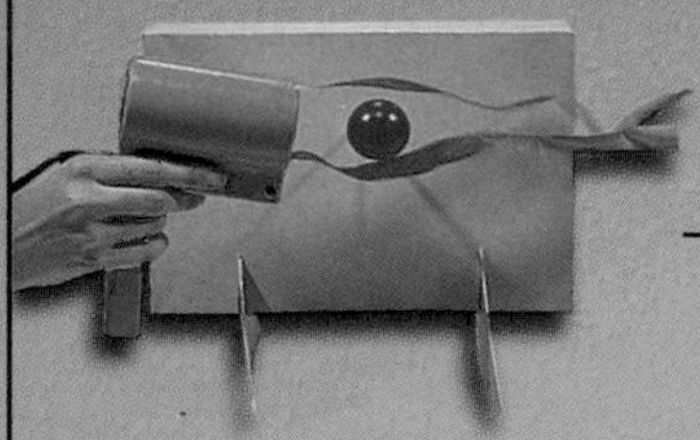

TESTING TIME

WHEN DESIGNERS ARE TESTING THE SHAPES OF NEW CARS, planes, and rockets, they use wind tunnels to see how air will pass over the shapes. Trails of smoke are blown over the objects to show this more easily. Build your own wind tunnel and test the shapes of different objects.

WHAT YOU NEED
Cardboard box
Sticks
Ribbons
Hair dryer

WIND TUNNEL

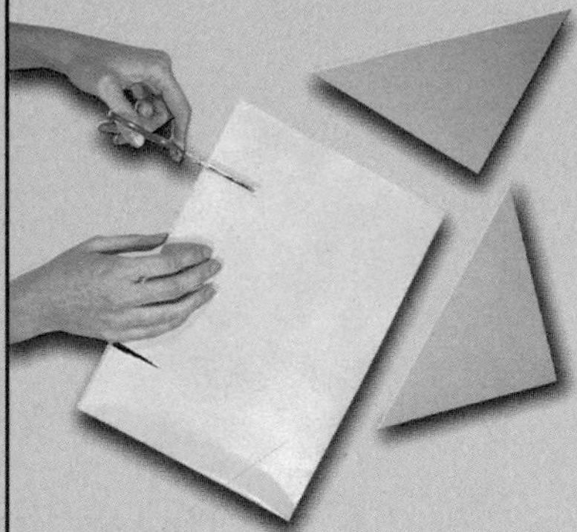

1 Make a backdrop for your wind tunnel using a cardboard box and two triangular bases.

2 Cut slits in the base of the box and slide the two bases in to hold the box upright.

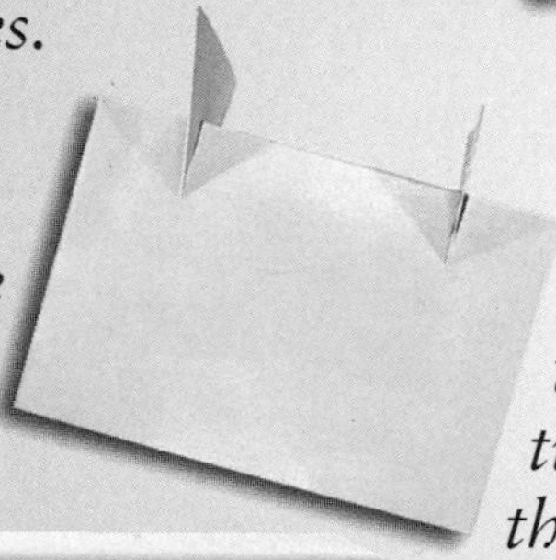

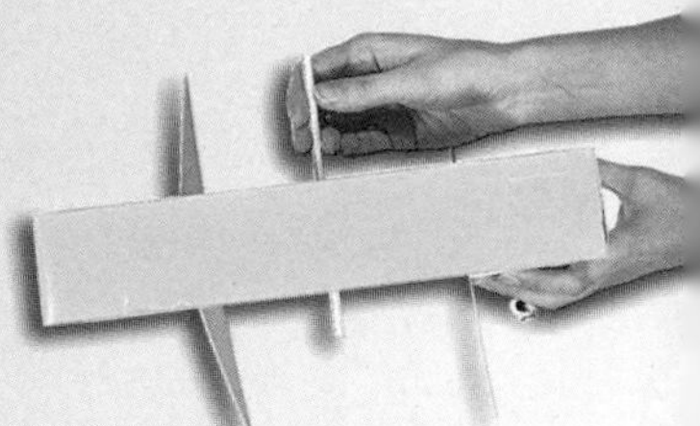

3 Carefully make holes in the center of the box and push two thin sticks through them. These sticks will support objects that you are testing in your wind tunnel.

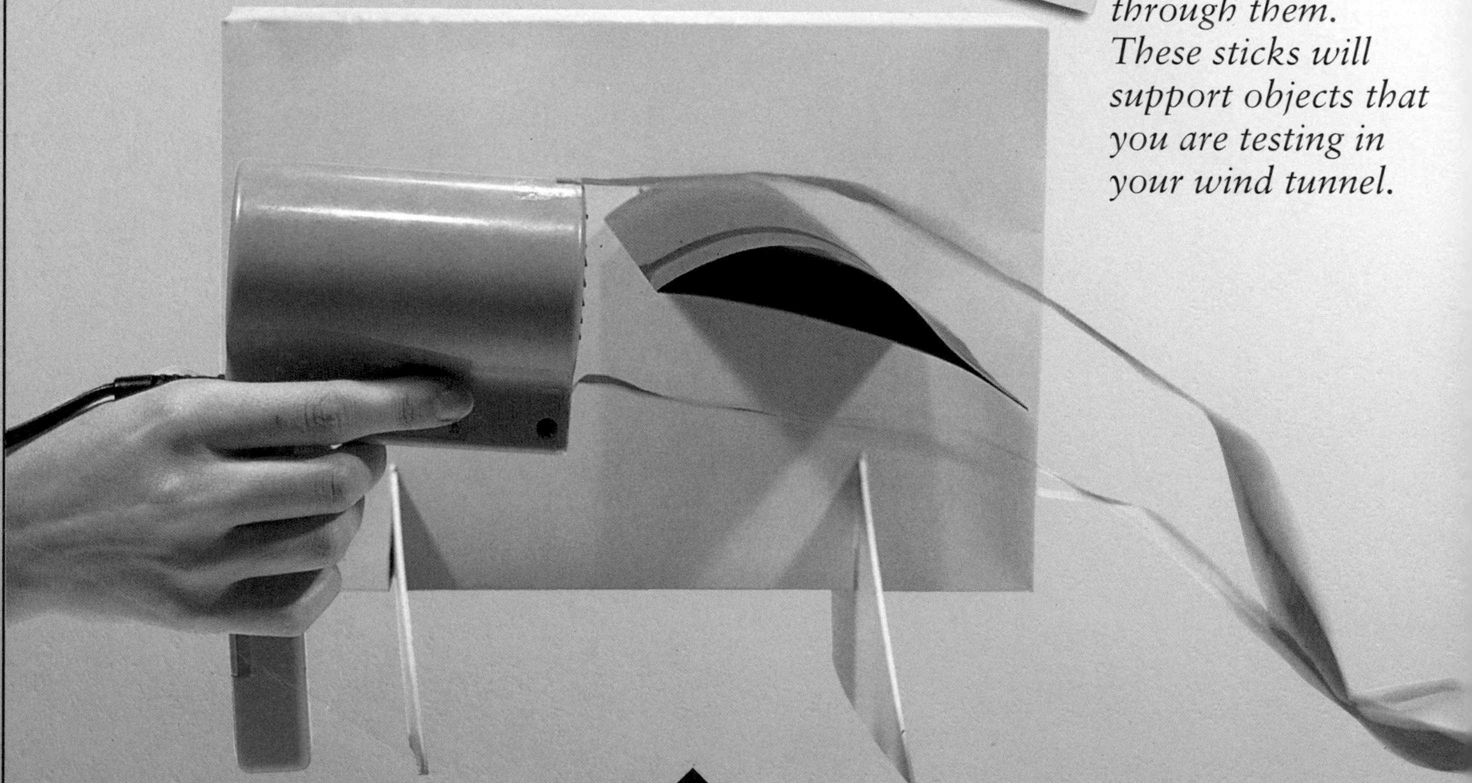

TESTING CARS

See how the two cars you used in the experiment on pages 18–19 test out in your wind tunnel.

WHY IT WORKS

The air will pass over streamlined objects easily without causing much drag (see pages 18–19). However, unstreamlined shapes, such as the ball, will disturb the air flow, making the ribbons flap around.

4 Fix two ribbons to each side of a hair dryer. With the dryer on "cool" setting, watch how the ribbons blow over a number of objects, such as a wing section (airfoil — see pages 22–23) and a ball.

WIND TUNNEL

AIRFOIL

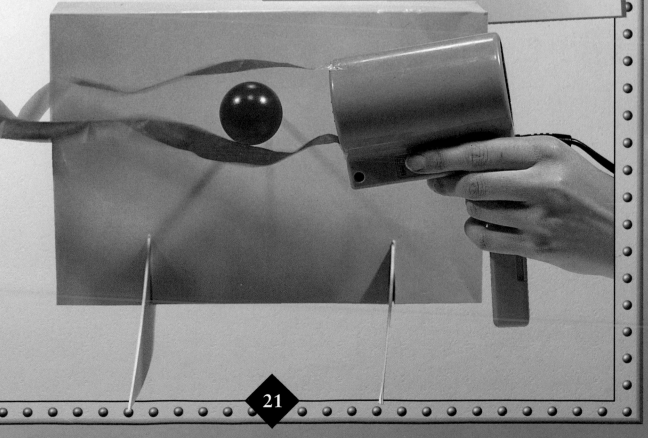

FLYING WINGS

BIRDS AND AIRCRAFT STAY IN THE AIR BECAUSE OF THE SHAPE OF THEIR WINGS. This special shape is called an airfoil. An airfoil is flat on the bottom and curved on the top. This experiment will show you how this shape causes a wing to rise as air passes over it.

AIRFOIL

1 Fold a rectangular piece of cardboard in two, leaving a slight overlap.

2 Push the overlapping ends together so that one side of the folded cardboard is now curved.

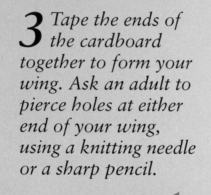

3 Tape the ends of the cardboard together to form your wing. Ask an adult to pierce holes at either end of your wing, using a knitting needle or a sharp pencil.

4 Now push a drinking straw through each pair of holes.

22

5 Pass lengths of thread through each straw and pull them tight. Fix them straight between a floor and a table. Make sure the curved edge of your wing is on top.

WHY IT WORKS

Because the wing is curved on top and flat underneath, air flowing over the wing has farther to travel — so it has to flow faster. Faster-flowing air has less pressure (see pages 16–17). The higher pressure below the wing then pushes the wing up.

6 Lift the wing a little and aim a hair dryer at the folded edge. Turn on the hair dryer, release the wing, and watch it rise.

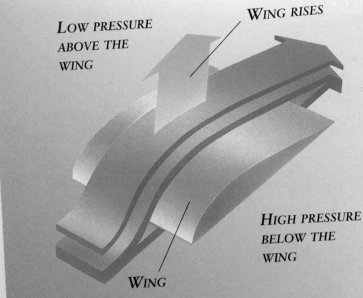

LOW PRESSURE ABOVE THE WING

WING RISES

HIGH PRESSURE BELOW THE WING

WING

BIGGER WINGS

Move the hair dryer away from the wing. The wing will not rise as easily.

LARGER AIRFOIL

FIRST AIRFOIL

You can also make a wing with a larger curved surface. This new wing will rise more easily because it creates more lift.

CONTROLLED FLIGHT

WHAT YOU NEED
Thin cardboard
Double-sided tape
Drinking straw
Thin stick
Modeling clay

BIRDS AND AIRCRAFT CAN FLY IN A CONTROLLED WAY because they have movable surfaces. Birds use their wings and tail feathers, while aircraft have flaps. Build your own glider and see how these movable surfaces can affect the flight of your aircraft.

ROLL, PITCH, AND YAW

Make your glider roll by moving the flaps on the wings. You can make your glider climb or dive (called pitch) by moving the flaps on the horizontal part of the tailplane. Make your glider move from side to side (yaw) by moving the flap on the upright part of the tailplane.

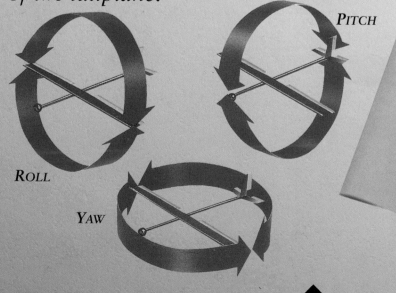

ROLL

PITCH

YAW

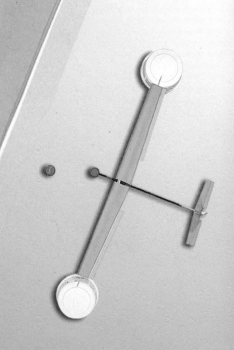

24

WHY IT WORKS

The lift created by the shape of the wings makes your glider fly. The movable surfaces turn the glider by deflecting the air as it flows over them. This deflected air pushes against the movable surfaces with enough force to alter the glider's course.

1 Cut out your wings and tailplane from cardboard in the shapes shown. Cut out some thin strips of cardboard, which will be stuck to the wings and the tailplane. These will make the movable surfaces.

2 Fold the wings over and tape together to make an airfoil shape (see pages 22–23). Feed a drinking straw through the wing to keep its airfoil shape. Fold the tailplane into shape so that it looks like a T when seen from the front.

3 Stick the thin strips of cardboard in place on the back of each wing and also on the back of all three parts of the tailplane. Stick the wing on a thin stick, which will act as the glider's body. Attach the tailplane to a piece of a drinking straw and tape this onto the back of the stick.

4 Your glider should balance if it is rested on two cups by its wings. Add a lump of modeling clay to your glider's nose and change the amount until the glider balances evenly. Now you can fly your glider.

CHAPTER 2

WATER & BOATS

INTRODUCTION

Water is amazing stuff! It comes in three different forms: as a solid, as a liquid, and as a gas. Water covers most of our planet. Some objects can float in it, other objects can sink in it, and a few objects can both float and sink in it! Water can be used to turn wheels, and it can even climb dozens of feet against the force of gravity! Find out more about freezing and melting, floating and sinking, and water power in this chapter.

CONTENTS

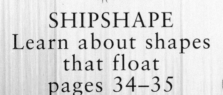

ICE AND WATER

IF LIQUID WATER IS COOLED ENOUGH, it turns into a solid lump. This solid form of water is called ice. Unlike most substances that shrink when they freeze, water gets larger, or expands, when it turns into ice. Because it expands, it becomes less dense, or lighter, than liquid water. This is why ice cubes float in a drink. This experiment will let you examine the different forms of water, and show you what happens when water freezes and when it melts.

WHAT YOU NEED
Plastic bottle
Food coloring
Ice-cube tray

MELTING ICEBERG

2 *The next day, carefully cut the top off the bottle. Fill with warm water from the faucet. Add a different food coloring and stir well.*

1 *Fill a clear plastic bottle with cold water. Add a few drops of food coloring and stir the mixture well. Pour the water into an ice-cube tray and leave it in the freezer overnight.*

WHY IT WORKS

As the ice melts, it turns into water. Because this melted ice is cooler than the warm water, it is also more dense. As a result, this freshly melted ice sinks. As it sinks it warms up, becomes less dense, and so rises again.

MELTING ICE WATER SINKS, IS WARMED, AND SO RISES IN A CIRCULAR CURRENT.

EXPANDING WATER

This experiment shows that water does expand when it freezes. Fill two plastic bottles with the same amount of water. Place one of them in the freezer overnight. Compare the two bottles the next day. The water placed in the freezer will have frozen and expanded.

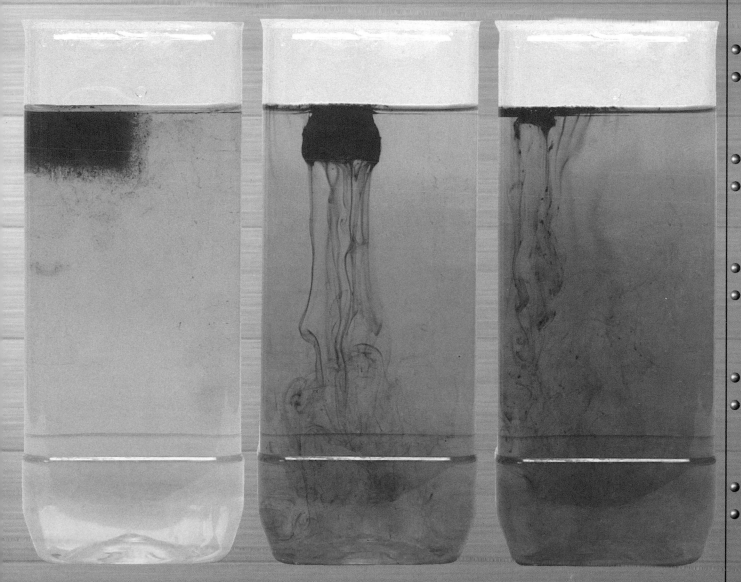

3 Drop one of the colored ice cubes into the warm water.

4 Watch the melting ice sink to the bottom of the bottle.

SINK AND SWIM

MOST OF THE WATER ON THE EARTH IS IN THE SEAS AND OCEANS. It is called salt water, because it contains salts and minerals that have been washed off the land. Because it contains these salty molecules, salt water is more dense than unsalty water, or freshwater. You can investigate the different densities of salt water and freshwater with this experiment.

WHAT YOU NEED
Salt, Potato
Colored cellophane
Food coloring
Two clear plastic bottles

FLOATING FISH

1 *Cut a thin slice from a potato to make the body of your fish. Cut out a semicircle and a triangular piece from some colored cellophane — these will form the fins and the tail.*

2 *Make a slit in the middle of your potato slice and push the cellophane semicircle through to make the fins above and below the body. Push the cellophane triangle into the back to make the tail.*

3 *Fill a bottle with cold water and add some salt. Stir this well until all of the salt has disappeared (dissolved). Keep adding salt until no more can dissolve. Pour into a clear plastic bottle from which the top has been cut.*

4 *Rinse and refill the first bottle with the same amount of water. Add some food coloring and stir well.*

GETTING THE SALT BACK

Ask an adult to boil the salt water in a pan. As the water boils away into steam, the salt is left behind in the pan in a white, crusty layer.

5 Slowly add the colored water to the salty water by pouring it over the back of a spoon. Place your fish carefully on the water's surface. Watch the fish sink through the colored water, but float on top of the salty water.

WHY IT WORKS

The salt water is more dense than the colored water, so it will stay at the bottom of the bottle, below the colored freshwater. Your fish is more dense, or heavier, than the colored freshwater, but less dense than the salt water. As a result, it will float between the two layers of water.

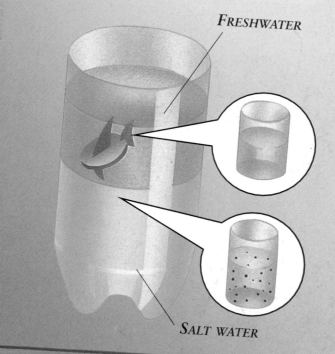

FRESHWATER

SALT WATER

OIL SLICK

JUST AS ICE FLOATS IN WATER BECAUSE IT IS LIGHTER, or less dense, so some liquids will float on the surface of water because they are also less dense. You may have noticed a film of oil floating on top of a puddle on a rainy day. This experiment lets you use floating oil paints to make patterns on paper.

You can make a swirling, multicolored pattern with oil-based paints and water.

SWIRLING PATTERNS

1 Mix some different colored oil-based paints with turpentine to make them thinner.

2 Fill a plastic bowl with cold water and carefully pour small amounts of the paints onto the surface.

3 Gently swirl the paints around using a clean stick.

4 Carefully lower a sheet of paper on top of the paint. Allow the paper to soak up some of the paint, then peel off the paper and see what patterns have been left on it by the paint.

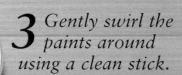

WHY IT WORKS

The paint floats on the surface of the water because it is less dense than the water. As a result, you can pick up the colors by placing your paper on top.

LIQUIDS OF DIFFERENT DENSITIES WILL FORM LAYERS IN A CONTAINER. OIL FLOATS ON TOP OF WATER BECAUSE IT IS LESS DENSE.

FLOATING STRAWS

A hydrometer is a device that measures density. You can make one using a drinking straw and some modeling clay. The hydrometer will float higher in dense liquids than in less-dense liquids.

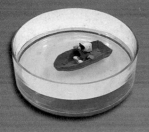

SHIPSHAPE

ENORMOUS AIRCRAFT CARRIERS AND LARGE CRUISE SHIPS float, yet a single metal screw will sink! When it comes to floating, size is not important. Instead, whether something floats or not depends on the weight of the water displaced by the object when it sits in the water. If this displaced water weighs more than the object, then the object will float.

WHAT YOU NEED
Modeling clay
Large bowl

CRAFTY VESSELS

1 Mold a lump of modeling clay into different solid shapes and see if they will float in a bowl of water.

2 Now roll the clay flat. Curve the edges up and pinch them together to form a boat shape. Make sure your boat doesn't leak!

3 Gently place your boat into the bowl of water and see if it floats. Mark on the side of your boat the level to which the water reaches.

4 Now make a clay figure to sit in the middle of your boat. Put the boat back in the water and you will see that the boat now sits lower in the water than when it was empty.

WHY IT WORKS

When you make your boat shape, the volume of water displaced by the boat weighs more than the boat, so it floats. When you add your clay passenger, you are increasing the weight of the boat, so it sinks slightly into the water.

FLOAT OR SINK?

Try making different boat shapes. A high-sided boat will float better than a shallow one. This is because it can sit lower in the water without having water spill over its sides. Now try some other boat shapes, and see which will carry the heaviest load.

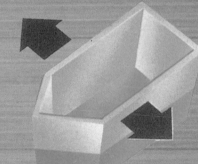

HIGH-SIDED BOAT

WATER FLOWS OVER SIDES OF BOAT

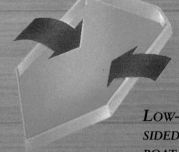

LOW-SIDED BOAT

REACHING THE DEPTHS

UNLIKE BOATS, SUBMARINES CAN SINK AND FLOAT as many times as they want. They do this by pumping air or water into special tanks inside them. If a submarine pumps water into these tanks, then it becomes heavier and sinks. If it pumps air into these tanks, then the submarine becomes lighter and rises toward the surface. Build your own submersible and see how it can sink and float as many times as you like!

WHAT YOU NEED

Drinking straw
Paper clip
Modeling clay
Plastic bottle

Squeeze the sides of the bottle and watch your submersible dive to the bottom. Release the bottle and your submersible will rise to the top.

BOTTLED SUBMERSIBLE

1 To make a submersible, cut the ribbed part off a flexible drinking straw and bend it in half.

2 Open up a metal paper clip and push each end into each end of the bent straw. Make sure that the paper clip will not slide out.

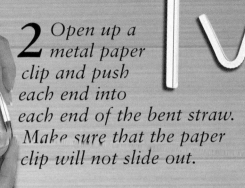

WHY IT WORKS

Trapped inside the straw is a bubble of air. When you squeeze the bottle, water is pushed into the straw and squashes the air bubble. As a result, your submersible becomes heavier and sinks.

3 Roll out three thin strips of modeling clay. Loop and pinch each one around the paper clip. These strips will weigh your submersible down.

4 Place your submersible in a glass of water to test that it floats the right way up. Alter the amount of modeling clay until it just floats.

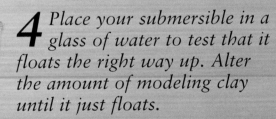

5 Place your submersible in a large plastic bottle full of water. Screw on the top securely.

UNDER PRESSURE

Stretch plastic wrap over the top of a tub of water and secure it with a rubber band. Push on the plastic — does your submersible still sink?

CLIMBING WATER

WHAT YOU NEED
Thin cardboard
Large bowl
Glue

HAVE YOU EVER WONDERED how plants can get water to every branch, stem, and leaf? This is due to a process called capillary action. It involves very long and very thin tubes that lie inside the plant. Forces inside these very narrow tubes actually draw water up. In the tallest trees, water can be pulled up dozens of feet!

CHANGING COLOR

Put some colored water in a vase of water with a flower. Over a couple of days the flower will draw the colored water up its stem and its flower will change color.

PAPER PETALS

1 Take a square piece of smooth writing paper or cardboard and fold it in half. Do not use shiny paper.

2 Now fold the paper in half again to form a square.

3 Fold it in half again, this time to form a triangle.

4 Cut the shape of a petal out of the side with the thickest fold. Unfold the paper and you will have your flower.

5 Using a pencil or a straw, roll the petals of the flower so that the petals remain closed.

6 Brighten up your flower by sticking a circle of different colored paper in the center. Make some other flowers of different shapes and colors.

7 Place your flowers in a bowl of water. Watch as the petals of your flowers unfurl as the water seeps into the paper.

WHY IT WORKS

Like the stem of a plant, the paper is full of tiny tubes called capillaries. An attractive force between the molecules of water and the sides of these tiny tubes is strong enough to draw water up. As the water rises, the paper becomes heavy and the petals unfurl.

WATER LEVEL

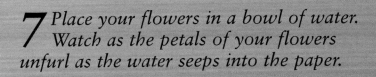

CAPILLARY TUBES IN PAPER

THE POWER OF WATER

UNLIKE AIR, LIQUIDS CANNOT BE SQUASHED. This makes liquids very useful in lifting heavy objects, from raising the bed of a dump truck to stretching the arm of a large digger. This use of liquids to lift and move objects is called hydraulics. Build your own hydraulic machine that will show you how water can be used to lift loads.

WHAT YOU NEED
Two plastic bottles
Drinking straws
Modeling clay
Balloon
Plastic cup
Food coloring

LIQUID LIFT

1 *Carefully cut the tops off two plastic bottles and make them the same height.*

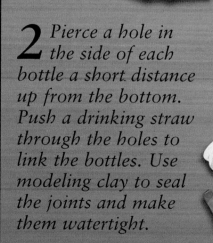

2 *Pierce a hole in the side of each bottle a short distance up from the bottom. Push a drinking straw through the holes to link the bottles. Use modeling clay to seal the joints and make them watertight.*

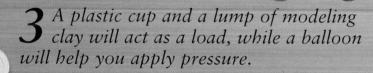

3 *A plastic cup and a lump of modeling clay will act as a load, while a balloon will help you apply pressure.*

4 *Color some water with food coloring and fill the bottles so that they are about two-thirds full. Float the cup in one bottle and place the lump of modeling clay in the cup.*

WHY IT WORKS

When you push down on the balloon, it forces water through the straw, transferring the force of your push into the other bottle. More water now sits in the other bottle, so the cup sits higher than it used to.

DOWNWARD FORCE

LOAD IS RAISED

UPWARD FORCE

5 Inflate the balloon a little, and place it in the other bottle. The balloon must press and slide against the bottle's sides. Now push down on the balloon, and watch the cup and the modeling clay rise in the other bottle.

CHANGING THE SYSTEM

Try using bottles of different sizes. You will find that a tall, narrow bottle will raise the load the highest because the displaced water has to fit into a narrower bottle.

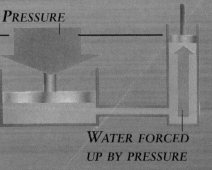

PRESSURE

WATER FORCED UP BY PRESSURE

WATERWORKS

WATER HAS BEEN USED as a source of power for thousands of years. Since Roman times, wooden waterwheels have powered millstones to grind corn into flour. Today, enormous dams channel fast-flowing water past the modern version of the wooden waterwheel — the turbine. This spins to make electricity.

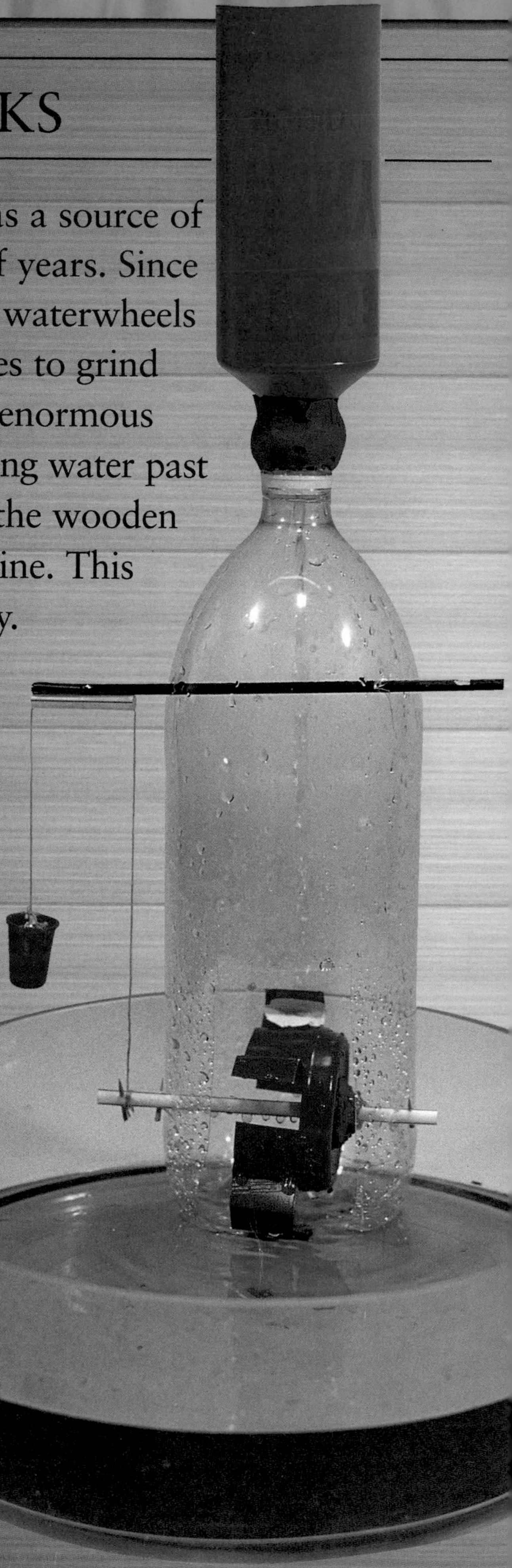

WHAT YOU NEED
Plastic bottles
Drinking straw
Tape, Stick
Toothpicks
Used matchstick
Modeling clay
Cotton thread
Large bowl
Bottle cap

Place the waterwheel in a bowl. Pour water into the upside-down bottle. Watch as water pours onto your waterwheel, causing it to spin and raise the bucket.

WHY IT WORKS

The waterwheel uses the energy of the falling water to make it spin. As it spins, the wheel winds up the thread, raising the bucket.

FALLING WATER SPINS THE WHEEL

WATER POWER

1 Cut the bottom off a liquid soap bottle to make your waterwheel. Cut out four flaps from the side of the wheel. Bend these flaps as shown to make the wheel's blades. Make a hole in the center of the wheel.

2 Cut a section out of the bottom of a plastic bottle, large enough for the wheel to fit into. Pierce holes on either side of this section.

GETTING HEAVY

Try adding small modeling-clay weights to the bucket. See how this affects the speed at which the bucket is lifted. You will find that with more weight to lift, the wheel will find it harder to raise the bucket. You could also try raising the height of the upside-down bottle — how does this affect the wheel?

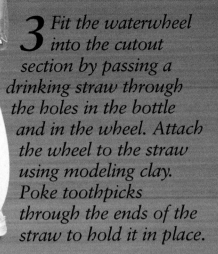

3 Fit the waterwheel into the cutout section by passing a drinking straw through the holes in the bottle and in the wheel. Attach the wheel to the straw using modeling clay. Poke toothpicks through the ends of the straw to hold it in place.

4 Pierce holes in the top of the plastic bottle and feed a stick through. Tape a length of drinking straw to one end of the stick.

5 Make a bucket using a bottle cap. Glue a match-stick across the top of the cap and tie a length of cotton thread to the matchstick. Feed the thread through the short straw and tie it around a toothpick pushed through the straw holding the waterwheel.

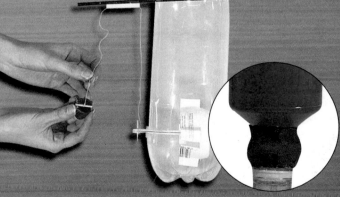

6 Fix another upside-down bottle on top, having cut off its bottom and sealed its top, leaving only a small hole.

PADDLING AWAY

WHAT YOU NEED
Small plastic drink bottle
Cardboard
Two sticks
Fruit-juice carton
Modeling clay
Rubber band

SOME OF THE EARLIEST POWERED BOATS WERE CALLED PADDLE STEAMERS. They used wheels, either at the rear of the boat or hung on its sides, to push the vessel through the water. However, the age of the paddle steamer was short-lived. Before long, boat builders found that propellers were better at pushing boats. Paddle steamers can still be seen today, but mostly as tourist attractions.

PADDLE POWER

1 Screw the top of a small plastic drink bottle on tightly. Cut a hole in the side of the bottle where the boat's funnel will sit.

2 Tape two sticks to the sides of the bottle so that they stick out past the bottom of the bottle.

3 Cut two rectangles from a fruit-juice carton, making sure that they are not as wide as the plastic bottle.

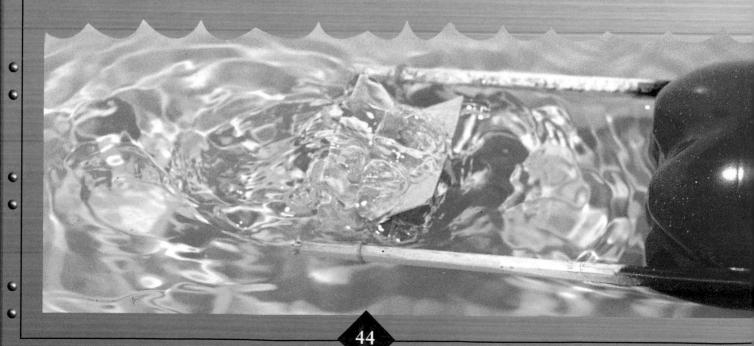

4 Make a slit halfway down each rectangle and slide the two together to form a cross-shaped paddle.

5 Tape a rubber band to the paddle and fix the ends of the band around the sticks. Make sure that the paddle does not touch the boat.

6 Weigh down the boat by placing a lump of modeling clay in the bottle. Cover the hole in the bottle with a cardboard funnel. Wind up the rubber band and place your boat in a bath of water. Watch as the paddle spins and the boat moves forward.

WHY IT WORKS

When you wind the rubber band, you are storing energy in it. This energy is released when you let go of the paddle, causing it to spin. As it spins, the blades push against the water, moving the boat forward.

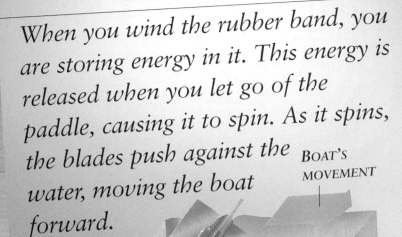

SPINNING PADDLE WHEEL

BOAT'S MOVEMENT

SIZE MATTERS

Try different sizes of paddle wheel on your boat. You will find that a larger wheel will push the boat along more quickly than a small one.

STEERING

WHAT YOU
NEED
Wire
Drinking straw
Fruit-juice
carton
Paddleboat
made on pages
44–45

FISH USE FINS ON THEIR BODIES TO STEER THEMSELVES THROUGH THE WATER. Similarly, boats have one fin at the rear that is used to steer — it's called a rudder. As well as a rudder, submarines have fins on their bodies, just like fish. They can use these fins to move the submarine up and down, as well as from side to side as it travels underwater.

By moving
your rudder from
side to side, you can make
your paddleboat alter its course.

WHY IT WORKS

The rudder works by deflecting the water, causing the boat to alter its course. If the rudder points straight back, then the boat will go straight on (1). If the rudder is turned to the right, then the boat will steer right (2) and left if the rudder is turned to the left (3).

1

2

3

SUBMARINE STEERING

Make a submarine out of a lump of modeling clay. Fix four fins to the sides, two at the front and two at the back. Adjust these fins to point up or down. See how they affect your submarine's descent through a bottle of water.

SUBMARINE
WITH FINS

RUDDER CONTROL

1 To make a rudder, bend a piece of wire to form a right angle, making the handle of your rudder.

2 Cut out a small square from a fruit-juice carton. Slide the wire through a length of straw and fix the square to the bottom of the wire. Fix the straw to the back of the paddle boat made on pages 44–45.

3 Wind up the paddle and place the boat in a tub of water. As the boat moves forward, turn the handle of the rudder from one side to the other, and see what this does to your boat's course.

CHAPTER 3

ELECTRICITY & BATTERIES

INTRODUCTION

What would we do without electricity? There would be no televisions, refrigerators, or computers — not even lightbulbs. This chapter looks at the basic aspects of electricity, as well as its more complex and practical uses. By following the projects, you will gain a greater understanding of circuits, switches, and conductors, and how we can use electricity.

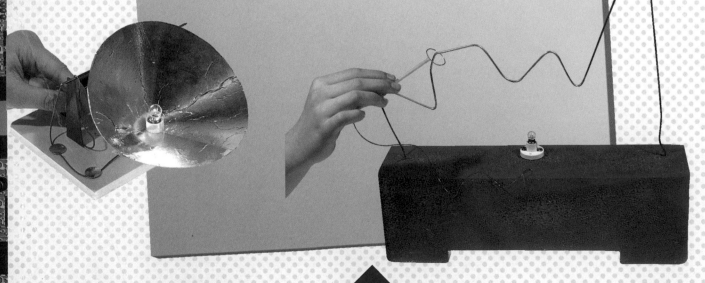

CONTENTS

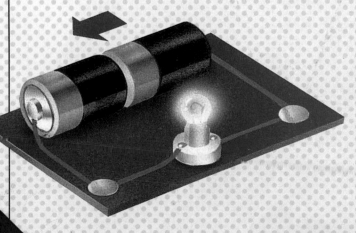

STATIC ELECTRICITY

THERE ARE TWO MAIN FORMS OF ELECTRICITY — static (still) and current (flowing). Some materials do not let electricity pass through them, but a static electrical charge is produced on their surface when they rub against certain other materials. When you take off your sweater, you may hear a crackling sound as you produce static electricity. Make frogs jump by static electricity.

WHAT YOU NEED
Tissue paper
Colored cardboard
Ping-Pong ball
String
Stick
Wool cloth
Scissors

FROLICKING FROGS

1 *Fold a piece of tissue paper a number of times and cut out the shape of a frog. This way you can cut out more than one frog at the same time.*

2 *Cut out two lily-pad shapes from green cardboard. Cut out some flowers, too. Put the lily pads on a piece of blue cardboard for the pond. Place the frogs on one lily pad.*

3 *Cut a bird shape out of yellow cardboard. Thread string through the bird and a Ping-Pong ball to join them together.*

4 *Tie the other end of the string to the end of the stick. Make sure the bird rests on top of the ball.*

5 *Rub the Ping-Pong ball against something made of wool. This gives it an electrical charge.*

WHY IT WORKS

The atoms that make up materials have negatively charged electrons and positively charged protons. When you rub the ball, you rub off electrons, leaving the ball with a positive charge. Because unlike charges attract each other, the positively charged ball attracts the paper frogs, which have a negative charge in relation to the ball.

STICKY BALLOONS

Rub a balloon against something wool. Hold it against a door or wall and let go. The balloon seems stuck to the door. It is held to the wall by static electricity. The charge slowly disappears. How long does the effect last?

6 Swing the bird and ball over the lily pond. Watch the frogs jump toward the bird. See if the frogs can leap to the other pad.

DETECTING A CHARGE

IN THE LAST PROJECT, we saw how static electricity can be made through rubbing. In 1895, an apparatus called a gold leaf electroscope was invented to detect static electrical charge. You can build an apparatus like a primitive electroscope that shows you if a material is charged with static electricity or not.

WHAT YOU NEED

Bare wire
Aluminum foil
Jar with cork lid
Thin foil candy wrapper
Balloon

PRIMITIVE ELECTROSCOPE

1 *Push a piece of wire through a large cork. Bend one end of the wire to make an "L" shape.*

2 *Roll a piece of aluminum foil into a ball and push it onto the top of the wire that's sticking out of the cork.*

WHY IT WORKS

Rubbing the balloon rubs off some of its electrons and makes it charged with static. When it comes close to the aluminum foil ball, electrons in the wrapper are attracted to the balloon and move toward it and into the aluminum ball. This leaves the metal foil in the jar positively charged. The two wings of foil try to repel each other and push apart, so the foil moves.

3 Fold a piece of thin foil from a candy wrapper in half and rest it on the bottom of the L-shaped wire. Put the cork in the jar, sealing the wrapper inside the jar.

4 Blow up a balloon and rub it on your shirt. Bring it close to the aluminum ball. Can you see the wrapper moving?

PUSHY BALLOONS

Blow up two balloons and rub them on a wool cloth to charge them. Then use thread to hang them up close to each other. Because you have rubbed electrons from the balloons onto the wool, the balloons are both positively charged. As a result, they repel one another and push apart.

A SIMPLE CIRCUIT

TODAY, WE CAN GENERATE large amounts of electricity. Metal wires and cables carry electricity from power plants to our homes. The electricity travels along these wires like water in a pipe. By switching on a light, you are completing one of these pathways, called a circuit. Electricity now flows through the light. The project below is fun to do, and it lets you set up your own circuit.

WHAT YOU NEED

6V lightbulb in socket
Insulated wire
Thin bare wire
Drinking straw
Two 1.5V batteries
Styrofoam block
Wire coat hanger, Tape

1 *Screw a small 6V lightbulb into a socket and attach a length of insulated wire to each side of the socket.*

2 *Make a piece of thin bare wire into a loop. Connect the loop and a long piece of insulated wire together. Thread a plastic drinking straw onto the wire and cover the joint with the straw to form a handle.*

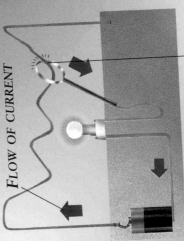

FLOW OF CURRENT

CIRCUIT IS COMPLETED

WHY IT WORKS

Electrons won't flow around the circuit until it is complete. Touching the loop to the wire hanger completes the circuit, and electrons flow, from the negative end of the battery around the wire to the positive end. The current flows in the opposite direction, and the bulb lights up.

3 Ask an adult to open up a wire coat hanger and bend it into bumps and curves. Attach one wire from the lightbulb to one end of the coathanger. Attach the other wire from the lightbulb to two batteries which have been taped together.

4 Attach the wire loop to the other end of the batteries. You can use modeling clay or tape to hold the wires on the ends of the batteries.

5 Thread the wire loop onto the free end of the hanger. Then stick the hanger into the styrofoam block. Try to move the loop along the coat hanger without their touching.

If you touch the coat hanger, the bulb will light up. See how far you can get!

SHORT CIRCUIT

Set up a simple circuit by connecting bare wires from the lightbulb to the battery. Then lay a metal object, such as a spoon, across the wires. The lightbulb goes out. You have made a short circuit.

SWITCHING ON

A SWITCHED CIRCUIT is a circuit where the flow of electricity is controlled by a switch. When the switch is open, or off, there is a gap in the circuit and the electricity doesn't flow. Electricity flows when the switch is closed, or on. In this project you can use switches to send messages to your friends using flashing lights to make the letters in code.

WHAT YOU NEED
Styrofoam boards
Modeling clay
*Two 6V lightbulbs
and sockets*
*Four 1.5V
batteries*
Insulated wire
Thumbtacks
Paper clips

SECRET MESSAGES

1 Put a lightbulb in each socket and attach the sockets to separate styrofoam boards. Connect the two sockets to each other with a long wire.

2 On each board, connect the sockets to a thumbtack holding a paper clip. Add another thumbtack within reach of each paper clip. These will be your switches.

3 On each board, connect the second thumbtack to one end of a battery. Now connect the other ends of the batteries to each other with a long piece of wire. Make sure that the two ends of the batteries which you are connecting are different. Otherwise, electricity will not flow.

MORSE CODE

You can send messages to a friend using Morse Code, by making the bulbs flash on and off quickly for dots and more slowly for dashes.

a	•–	s	•••
b	–•••	t	–
c	–•–•	u	••–
d	–••	v	•••–
e	•	w	•––
f	••–•	x	–••–
g	––•	y	–•––
h	••••	z	––••
i	••	1	•––––
j	•–––	2	••–––
k	–•–	3	•••––
l	•–••	4	••••–
m	––	5	•••••
n	–•	6	–••••
o	––•	7	––•••
p	•––•	8	–––••
q	––•–	9	––––•
r	•–•	0	–––––

4 *When the paper clip switches are touching the thumbtacks, the bulbs will light up. Keep one switch closed, and open and close the other to send a signal down the wire.*

WHY IT WORKS

When the paper clips are in contact with the thumbtacks, the circuit is complete and electrons can flow, lighting the bulbs. To send a signal down the wire, the sender must raise and lower one of the paper clips to open and close the circuit. This is shown by the lightbulbs going on and off.

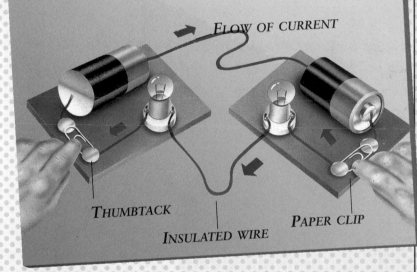

FLOW OF CURRENT

THUMBTACK

INSULATED WIRE

PAPER CLIP

LIGHTING THE DARK

WHAT YOU NEED
Glue, Pen
Lightbulb in
socket
Insulated wire
Colored paper
and cardboard
Brass fasteners
Battery

IN 1879, AMERICAN INVENTOR Thomas Edison made the first electric lightbulb. For the filament, the part that glows when electricity is passed through it, he used a piece of cotton thread heated to a black strip. He removed the air from the lightbulb and turned on the current. The lightbulb glowed. By 1913, a metal called tungsten was used as the filament.

ELECTRONIC QUIZ

1 Make up some questions and answers, and write each on a separate piece of paper.

2 Glue the questions in one column to one side of a piece of cardboard. Glue the answers in random order in another column on the cardboard.

3 Push a brass paper fastener through the cardboard next to each question and each answer.

4 On the back of the cardboard, join the brass fastener of each question with a short length of wire to its correct answer.

5 Make a circuit with more wire, a battery, and a lightbulb. Leave the ends of the wires free.

TRAFFIC LIGHTS

Build a circuit with three colored lights to make traffic lights. Connect them together with switches so they can be turned on in different sequences depending on whether the traffic must stop or go

6 Ask a friend a question and let him or her choose one of the answers. With the free ends of the wires in your circuit, touch the paper fasteners next to the question and the answer your friend gives. If the bulb lights up, the answer is correct.

WHY IT WORKS

Each question's paper fastener is connected by wire to the paper fastener of the correct answer. By touching the wires of your circuit to a question and its answer, you complete the circuit, so electricity flows and the bulb lights up. If the answer is wrong, the circuit is not completed, and the bulb will not light up.

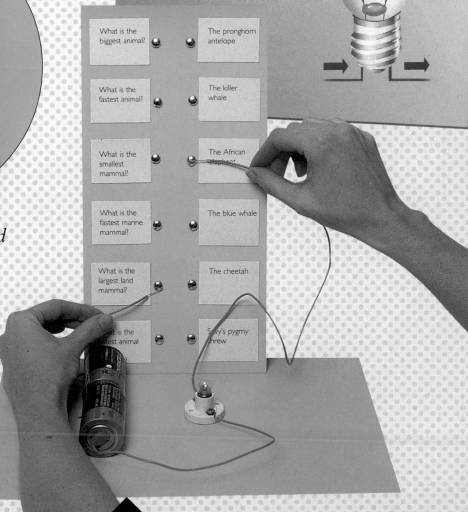

What is the biggest animal?

The pronghorn antelope

What is the fastest animal?

The killer whale

What is the smallest mammal?

The African elephant

What is the fastest marine mammal?

The blue whale

What is the largest land mammal?

The cheetah

What is the fastest animal

Savy's pygmy shrew

CONDUCTORS

SOME MATERIALS WILL NOT ALLOW ELECTRICITY to flow along them. They are called insulators. Other materials will let a current pass through them. They are called conductors. We need conductors to make electric wires and circuits, while insulators are important in protecting us from dangerous electric currents. This project will show you the difference between conductors and insulators.

WHAT YOU NEED
Thick colored cardboard
Aluminum foil
Insulated wire
Adhesive vinyl
Two batteries
Lightbulb in socket
Nail

3 *Before you stick down a final conducting path, make a hole near the edge of the board and insert the end of some insulated wire.*

ELECTRIC MAZE

1 *Cut a piece of aluminum foil the same size as your board. Cover the foil with a sheet of clear adhesive vinyl.*

2 *Design your maze on the board, and cut out strips of the vinyl-covered foil to fit your paths. Attach them plastic side up. These are your insulated paths.*

4 *Attach the other end of the wire to a battery. To the other terminal of the battery, attach a wire leading to a lightbulb in a socket. Attach another piece of wire to the other side of the socket and put a nail on the end of it.*

TESTING

You can test other materials to see if they are conductors using your circuit. Touch the free ends of the wires to the ends of objects made from different materials, such as erasers and spoons.

WHY IT WORKS

When the nail touches the plastic, the lightbulb goes out. The vinyl is an insulator and blocks the current. The electrons in an insulator are not free to move as they are in a conductor, such as aluminum foil, so the current doesn't flow.

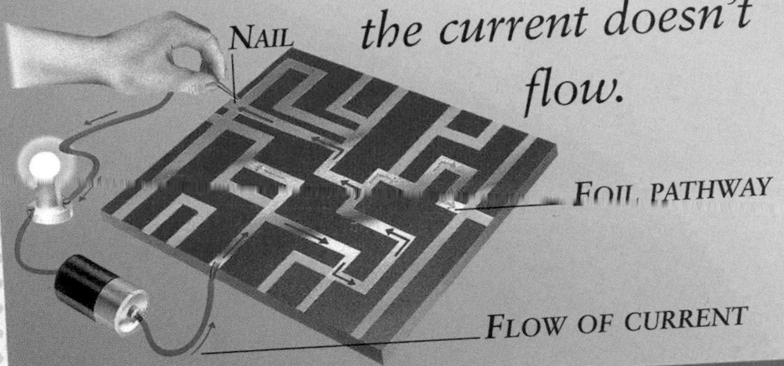

NAIL

FOIL PATHWAY

FLOW OF CURRENT

5 Cut out your final conducting path and stick it to your board, foil side up. Make sure the wire contacts the foil (but not its vinyl cover) at one end. Let your friends find their way through the maze.

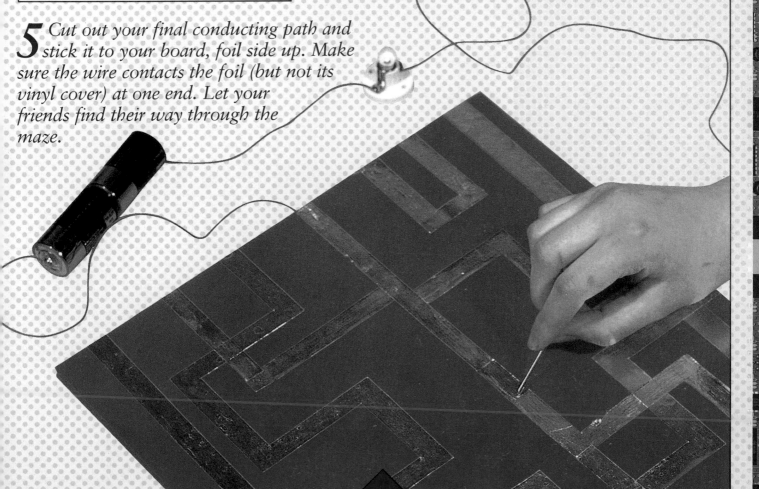

POOR CONDUCTORS AND RESISTORS

NOT ALL CONDUCTORS ARE EQUAL. An electrical current can pass through some more easily than others. The thinner the wire, the higher the resistance, like the slower flow of water through pipes of different widths. Resistance also varies with length. In the experiment below you can test different conductors to see if they have high or low resistance.

WHAT YOU NEED
Lightbulb in socket
Insulated wire
Thick board
Cardboard
Paper clip
Pencil lead
1.5V batteries
Thumbtacks
Aluminum foil

WOOD

Replace the lead in the experiment with a wooden skewer that has been soaked in salt water overnight. The salt in the water should allow the wood to conduct electricity. As the wood begins to dry out, the resistance will increase until eventually the wood will stop conducting.

RESISTANCE

1 Set up a circuit like the one shown, using insulated wire, thumbtacks, and a lightbulb in a socket. Get some lead from a self-propelling pencil, and cut out two pieces of cardboard to rest it on.

2 To reflect the light, make a shade from a cardboard disk and aluminum foil.

3 Cut a slit in the disk and glue it into a cone shape. Cut a hole in the center of the cone, then place it over the lightbulb.

4 Glue the cardboard supports upright on the board, as shown. Slip the paper clip over the end of the pencil lead and lay the lead on the cardboard supports.

5 Attach the end of one of your wires to the end of a battery. Connect another piece of wire to the other end of the battery. Add the paper clip over the lead to the end of this wire. Attach the end of your other free wire to the end of the pencil lead.

WHY IT WORKS

Resistance increases the farther the current has to travel. As the paper clip moves toward the battery end, the distance the current has to move is shortened, so there is less resistance and the lightbulb glows more brightly.

PENCIL LEAD

FLOW OF CURRENT

MOVEMENT OF PAPER CLIP

VOLTAGE AND CIRCUITS

IF YOU PUT MANY LIGHTBULBS in a circuit in a line, one after the other, they are said to be in series. If one of the lightbulbs goes out, they all go out. Streetlights in the early 1900s were set up like this, and streets were plunged into darkness when one of the lights failed. The solution was to put them in parallel, so the current didn't have to go through one lightbulb to get to another. Streetlights today are in parallel circuits, so that if one lightbulb fails, the others will continue to glow.

WHAT YOU NEED
Two large boards
Thumbtacks
Insulated wire
3V lightbulbs in sockets
1.5V batteries

WHY IT WORKS

A series circuit uses one path to connect the lightbulb to the battery. If two batteries are used, the lightbulb glows twice as brightly. Two lightbulbs in a series circuit glow less brightly than one. A parallel circuit has more than one path for the current. Each lightbulb receives the current at the same force, or voltage, no matter how many lightbulbs there are in parallel. If a lightbulb burns out, the others continue to glow because their circuits are not broken.

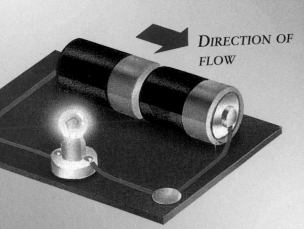

DIRECTION OF FLOW

SERIES AND PARALLEL

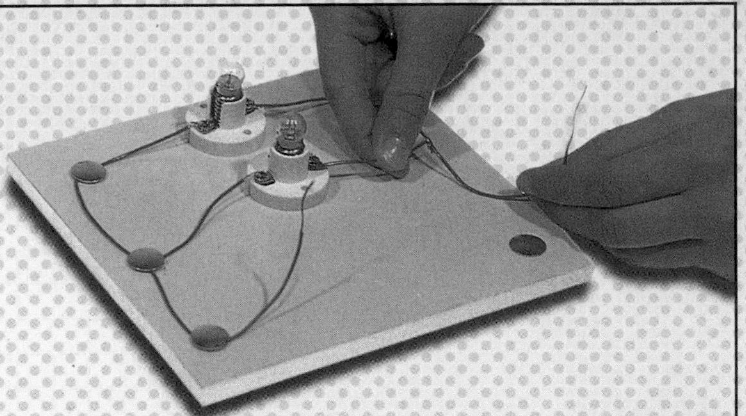

1 Set up a circuit with two lightbulbs in parallel, connecting the bare ends of the wires to thumbtacks as shown. Attach the free ends of the wire to the ends of a battery. Both lightbulbs glow with equal brightness.

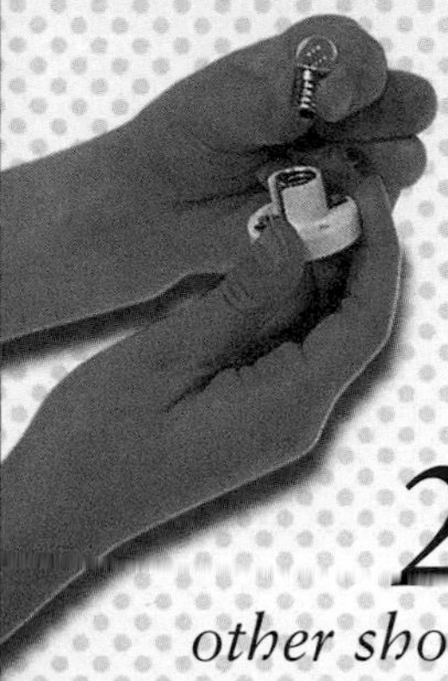

2 Now remove one of the lightbulbs. The other should still be alight.

3 Now set up a circuit with two batteries connected end to end, in series. Connect them to a single lightbulb. How brightly does it glow? Take one of the batteries out. How brightly is the lightbulb glowing now?

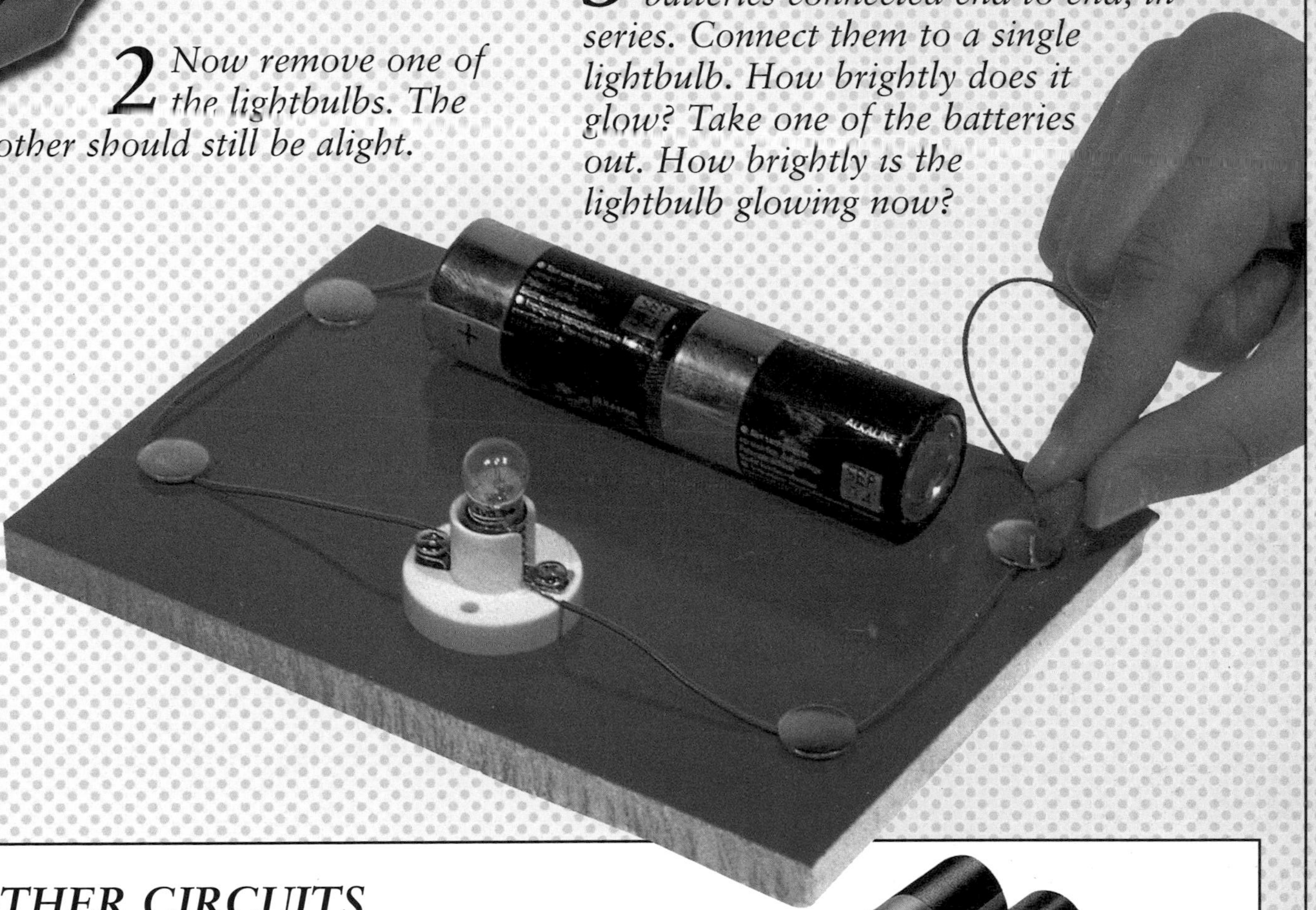

OTHER CIRCUITS

Using the parallel circuit that you made in the project, replace the bulb in the middle of the circuit with a battery, as shown here. How does this affect the lightbulb? Does it glow brighter or dimmer? Or does it not glow at all?

ELECTRICITY AND IONS

AN ELECTRICAL CURRENT can pass through liquids, such as a salt solution, causing a chemical reaction. This is called electrolysis. Two metal plates, called electrodes, deliver the current to the solution (electrolyte).

Electrolysis is used to coat metallic objects with a thin layer of a more expensive, attractive, or hard-wearing metal. This process is called electroplating.

WHAT YOU NEED

Glass jar of salt water
Copper coin
Paper clip
Two batteries
Insulated wire
Modeling clay

ELECTROPLATING

1 Connect the two batteries with the unlike terminals touching. Connect insulated wire to the free terminals. Attach the copper coin to the wire from the positive battery terminal.

2 Attach a paper clip to the wire from the negative battery terminal. Fill the jar with water, add salt, and place the coin and the paper clip in the water. They will act as the electrodes.

SALT AND VINEGAR

Try the experiment again using a solution of salt dissolved in vinegar. Do you notice any difference? Does anything happen to the paper clip? Add more batteries in parallel to increase the "pressure" of the current.

WHY IT WORKS

The electricity flows through the solution as charged particles called ions. Copper ions carry the positive charge toward the negative paper clip, where they pick up electrons and are deposited on the paper clip as a thin layer of copper.

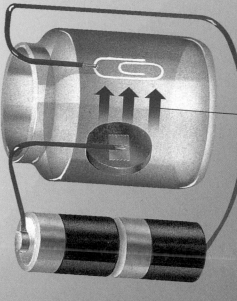

CURRENT FLOWS THROUGH THE SOLUTION, CARRYING COPPER IONS TO THE PAPER CLIP

3 Watch closely to see what happens. Are there bubbles forming? Leave the coin and the paper clip for a few minutes before taking them out. Are there any color changes? Put them back in the water for a while longer. Can you see any more changes?

CHAPTER 4

MAGNETISM & MAGNETS

INTRODUCTION

Magnetism is all around us. We use it daily, from speaking on the telephone to navigating ships around the oceans. In this chapter, we look at the basic aspects of magnetism, its practical uses, and also those that are more complex. Try the projects and learn more about the world of magnetic fields, compasses, motors, and electromagnets. Read on and find out how magnets work.

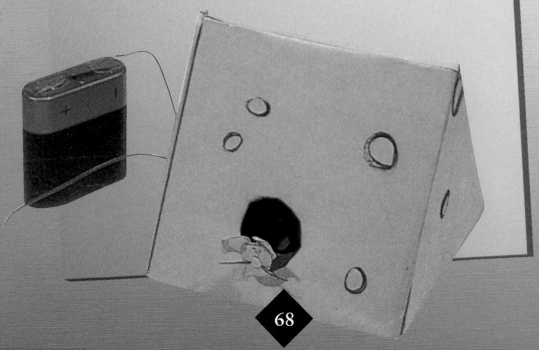

CONTENTS

METALS AND MAGNETS

MANY SUBSTANCES ARE METALS, such as iron, aluminum, copper, and gold. But only a few metals are magnetic — able to attract and repel other magnetic substances. The main magnetic metal is iron. Treasure hunters use magnetic metal detectors to find magnetic metallic objects. Build your own metal detector in the project below.

WHAT YOU NEED

Cardboard
Glue
Stick
Button magnet
Modeling clay
Flowerpot tray full of sand
Colored paper
Magnetic and nonmagnetic objects

HIDDEN TREASURE

1 Cut out a cardboard circle 4 inches across and cut a slit from the edge to the center. Overlap and glue the two ends to make a cone. Push the end of a stick through the center for a handle. Attach a button magnet inside the cone with modeling clay.

2 Wind strips of paper around the stick and glue them to the cone to hold it in place. Decorate the cone with colored strips of paper.

WHY IT WORKS

A magnet is made up of tiny magnetic parts called domains that are all pointing in the same direction. Other metals also have domains, but they point in many directions. A magnet makes the domains in ferrous (iron-based) metal line up. The metal becomes magnetized.

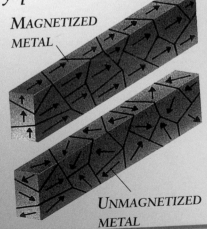

MAGNETIZED METAL

UNMAGNETIZED METAL

3 Cover the bottom of a shallow flowerpot tray with sand. Bury some magnetic and some nonmagnetic objects in the sand.

MAGNETIC MATERIALS

Collect as many different materials as you can find. First guess which ones you think are magnetic and which ones aren't. Then test them against a magnet. Were you right? Did any of the objects surprise you?

4 Move your metal detector slowly over the sand. Hold it at different heights to discover how low to hold it to find objects.

MAGNETIC FIELDS

EVERY MAGNET HAS AREAS WHERE ITS MAGNETIC FORCE IS STRONGEST. These areas are called poles. Every magnet has at least two poles, depending on its shape. The poles are named north and south. Surrounding every magnet is a magnetic field. This is created by lines of force going between the poles. This project shows you these lines of force.

WHAT YOU NEED
Two bar magnets
Large sheet of paper
Iron filings
2 Thin books

FIELD EXPERIMENT

WHY IT WORKS

Lines of magnetic force run from pole to pole. They are strongest near the poles, where they are closest together. The iron filings are drawn to the magnetic field and show the lines of force. They concentrate around the poles where the lines of force meet.

NORTH

SOUTH

LINES OF FORCE

1 *Ask a grown-up to make some iron filings by filing down an iron nail.*

FIELD PATTERNS

You can repeat this experiment with as many differently shaped magnets as you can find. How do their field patterns vary? Try to guess the shape of the magnetic field of a magnet by the shape of the magnet itself.

2 Place two bar magnets on a table top, with unlike poles facing each other, between two books. Lay the paper across the two books over the magnets. Scatter the iron filings on the paper. Tap the paper and watch the iron filings line up along the magnetic fields.

PUSHING AND PULLING

WHEN TWO METAL OBJECTS PULL, or attract, each other it is difficult to tell if both of them are magnets. The real test is to see if they push, or repel, each other. The south pole of one magnet seeks the north pole of another magnet and repels the other's south pole. Test this out in the bumblebee project below.

BUMBLEBEE

1 Ask an adult to cut a Ping-Pong ball in half. Paint the outside with the black and yellow stripes of a bee. Add some paper wings, eyes, and feelers.

2 Place a button magnet inside the bee using modeling clay, with one of its poles facing down.

3 Glue two sticks together to make a frame. Make a hole in an upside-down flowerpot tray and insert the longer stick. Hold it firmly in place with some modeling clay.

4 Cover a bar magnet in brown paper for the stem of the flower. Stand it upright in the center of the base with modeling clay, with the pole that repels the bee on top.

ZOOMING IN

Turn the flower's magnet stem upside down so that opposite, or unlike, poles are facing each other; the bee is now attracted to the flower. Let the bee swing. How long does it swing?

74

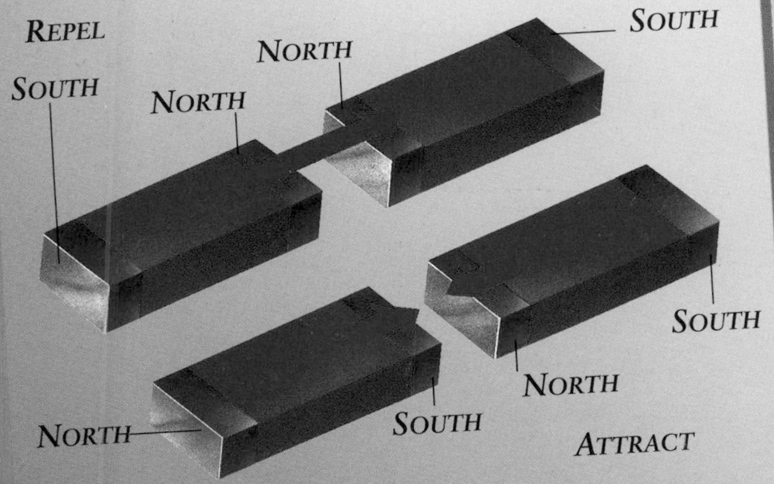

5 Cut out some petals from colored paper and make a large flower. Attach it to the top of the bar magnet stem.

6 Suspend the bee from the frame with a piece of thread.

7 Swing the bee over the flower and watch it buzz around the flower. Does it ever come to rest?

WHY IT WORKS

The poles facing each other in this project are the same, or like, poles; they strongly repel each other. This makes the bee swing for a very long time because the flower is pushing the bee away all the time. Only two magnets can repel each other like this.

REPEL

SOUTH

NORTH

NORTH

SOUTH

NORTH

NORTH

SOUTH

SOUTH

NORTH   ATTRACT

SOUTH

HOMEMADE MAGNET

YOU CAN MAKE YOUR OWN MAGNETS FROM NEEDLES AND PAPER CLIPS. Then you can test them by seeing if they attract and repel one another (see the project on pages 74–75). Magnets made from iron slowly lose their magnetic effect over time. Magnets made from steel are permanent magnets.

WHAT YOU NEED
Needle
Paper clip
Shallow dish
Styrofoam
Magnet

MAKING A MAGNET

1 *Stroke one end of a paper clip with the south pole of a magnet, at least twenty times. Always stroke the paper clip in the same direction, and lift it well clear at the end to start a new stroke. This end will be the north pole of the paper clip.*

2 *Tape the paper clip to a piece of styrofoam shaped like a boat, with the north pole pointing toward the front. Float it in a shallow dish of water.*

WHY IT WORKS

Magnets push and pull each other because opposite poles attract one another and like poles repel one another. This attraction and repulsion is strong enough to move the styrofoam boat through the water. When the north pole of the needle is brought close to the north pole of the paper clip, the paper clip is pushed away. This force is so strong it is sometimes almost impossible to push two magnets together.

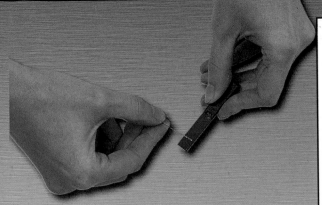

3 Stroke the eye of the needle with the north pole of the magnet. This magnetizes the needle, making the eye the south pole of the needle and the point the north pole.

4 Bring the eye of the needle near the end of the paper clip. The front of the boat turns toward the needle.

5 Turn the needle around and bring its point near the end of the paper clip. The boat turns away from the needle.

BOUNCING MAGNETS

Place a piece of wood between two magnets with like poles on top of each other. Tape the magnets together and remove the wood. The two magnets repel each other, but the tape keeps them in place. Press down on the top magnet and see it spring back or twist because of the repulsion. This is how a Maglev (magnetic levitation) train works.

Traveling Magnetism

MAGNETIC FORCE CAN TRAVEL THROUGH MANY MATERIALS, EVEN WATER. Divers use an instrument called a magnetometer to uncover treasure on the ocean floor. You have seen a magnetic field travel through paper to iron filings (see pages 72–73). What other materials do you think magnetic fields can travel through? This project shows that magnetism is not stopped by nonmagnetic materials.

WHAT YOU NEED
Colored cardboard
Two sticks
Ping-Pong ball
Two bar magnets
Two small magnets
Cardboard lid
Adhesive tape

CORK BOBBING

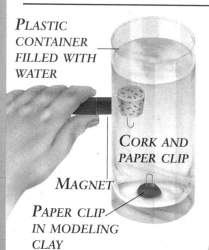

PLASTIC CONTAINER FILLED WITH WATER

CORK AND PAPER CLIP

MAGNET

PAPER CLIP IN MODELING CLAY

Cut the top off a plastic bottle. Attach a paper clip to the bottom. Fill the bottle with water. Push a paper clip into a cork to make a hook. Use a bar magnet to drag the cork beneath the water and hook it to the paper clip at the bottom.

MAGNETIC HOCKEY

1 Cut out two cardboard figures holding hockey sticks. Paint them with team colors. Tape a magnet onto each hockey stick.

2 Tape bar magnets to the end of two long sticks for moving your players. Check that the poles of the magnets attract one another.

3 Make the rink from an upside-down cardboard lid. Set the lid on four wooden legs. Make the goals out of strips of cardboard. Mark the center with colored tape or paint.

WHY IT WORKS

Some nonmagnetic materials allow magnetic force to pass through them without being affected. Magnets on either side of a piece of cardboard still attract or repel each other. The thicker the material or the further apart the magnets are, the weaker the magnetic force.

CARDBOARD

HOCKEY-STICK MAGNET

SOUTH POLE OF HOCKEY-STICK MAGNET

NORTH POLE OF MAGNET UNDER CARDBOARD

MAGNET

4 Place the players on the "ice" and move them using the sticks with the magnets under the ice. Use a Ping-Pong ball to score goals.

MAGNETIC EARTH

THE EARTH BEHAVES LIKE A GIANT MAGNET. It produces a magnetic field and has two poles. Its magnetic poles are not in exactly the same place as its true poles. A compass needle has been magnetized and points to the earth's magnetic north pole. In the project below you can show how the earth acts as a big magnet.

WHAT YOU NEED
Colored cardboard
Five compasses
Bar magnet
Glue

ORIENTEERING

Orienteering means finding your way across the land with a map and a compass. The compass needle points to magnetic north. As you read your map you have to make an adjustment to your compass reading to find true north.

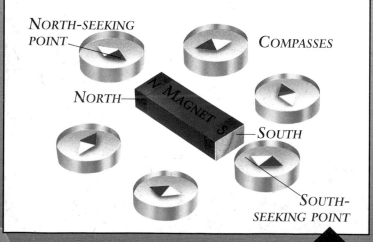

NORTH-SEEKING POINT

COMPASSES

NORTH

N MAGNET S

SOUTH

SOUTH-SEEKING POINT

FROM POLE TO POLE

1 Cut out a circle of blue cardboard. Draw the map of the world onto cardboard of a different color. Stick it onto the blue circle. This is your earth.

2 You will need five compasses to lay around the outside of your map.

3 Lay the bar magnet under your map, with the north pole at the top and the south pole at the bottom.

WHY IT WORKS

The needles of the compasses follow the lines of magnetic force of the bar magnet. The same kind of field exists around the earth. In the top half of your map, the compass needles point to the north pole of the magnet and the miniature earth.

NORTH POLE

SOUTH POLE

4 Position each compass as shown here, with the north of the compass dial pointing north. The needles move to follow the lines of force of the bar magnet under your map.

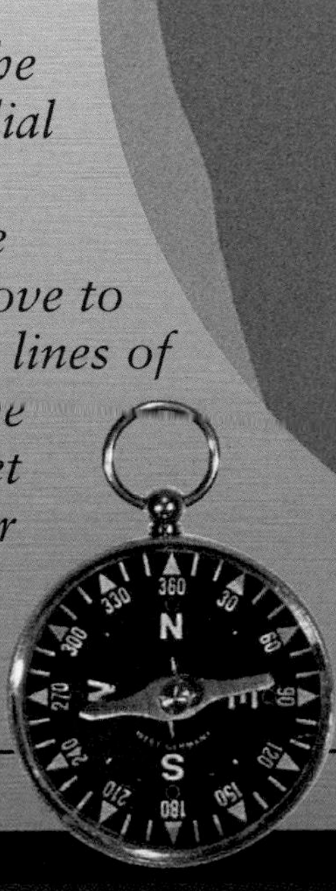

COMPASS BEARINGS

WHAT YOU NEED

Shallow dish
Cork
Magnet
Steel needle

IN THE PREVIOUS PROJECT, WE SAW HOW THE EARTH ACTS LIKE A GIANT MAGNET. Chinese and Mediterranean sailors started to use magnetic compasses about 1,000 years ago. These first compasses were little more than magnetized pieces of iron floating on cork in bowls of water (see pages 76–77). You can make your own compass.

MAKE A COMPASS

1 Half-fill a shallow dish with water. Magnetize a steel needle by stroking one end of a magnet along its length at least 50 times. Always stroke the needle in the same direction and lift it well clear of the magnet at the end to start a new stroke.

ALTERNATIVE COMPASS

Any magnet or magnetized object will align itself with the earth's magnetic field if it is allowed to swing freely. You can make a different compass by balancing a magnetized needle on a fold of paper on top of an upright stick. Cover this delicate compass with a see-through container to keep any wind from blowing it off and it will swing around to seek north.

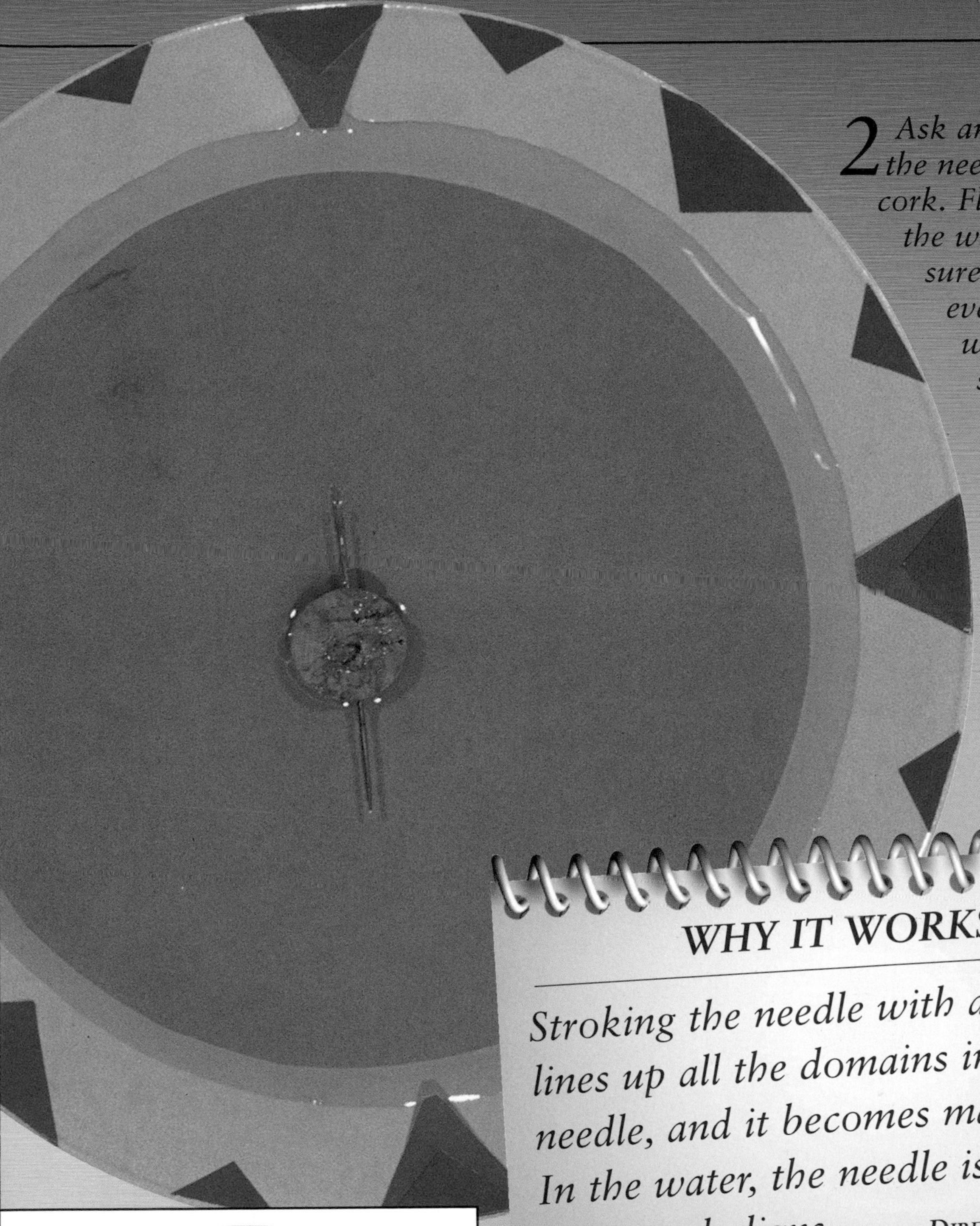

2 *Ask an adult to push the needle through a cork. Float the cork in the water, making sure it balances evenly. As the water becomes still again, the needle will swing around to seek the earth's magnetic north pole.*

WHY IT WORKS

Stroking the needle with a magnet lines up all the domains in the needle, and it becomes magnetized. In the water, the needle is free to move and aligns itself with the earth's magnetic field.

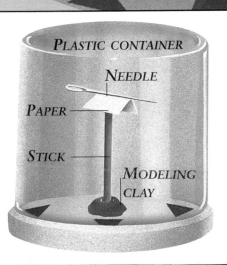

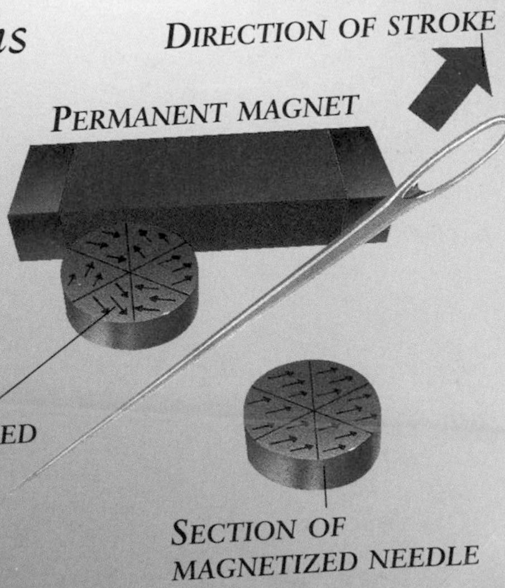

PLASTIC CONTAINER
NEEDLE
PAPER
STICK
MODELING CLAY

DIRECTION OF STROKE
PERMANENT MAGNET
SECTION OF UNMAGNETIZED NEEDLE
SECTION OF MAGNETIZED NEEDLE

ELECTROMAGNETS

WHAT YOU NEED
Cardboard
Cardboard boxes
Spool, Pencil
Insulated wire
Iron nail
Battery
Paper clip
Thumbtacks

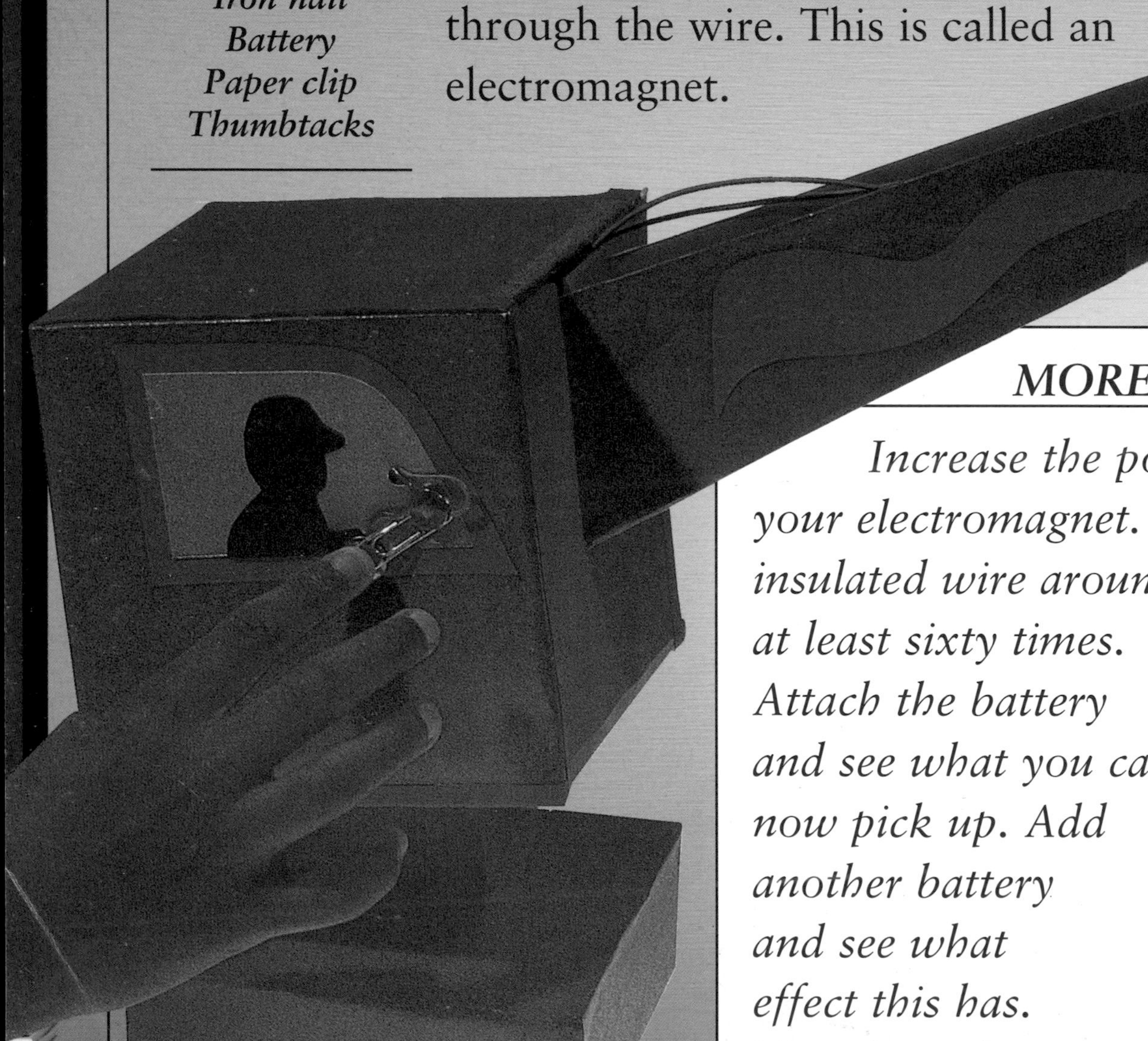

THE RELATIONSHIP BETWEEN ELECTRICITY AND MAGNETISM WAS DISCOVERED IN THE 1800s. The Danish physicist Hans Christian Oersted discovered that an electric current running through a wire produces a magnetic field. By coiling the wire around a soft iron bar, the iron bar becomes magnetized as long as the current is running through the wire. This is called an electromagnet.

MORE POWER

Increase the power of your electromagnet. Wrap the insulated wire around the nail at least sixty times. Attach the battery and see what you can now pick up. Add another battery and see what effect this has. How long does the battery last?

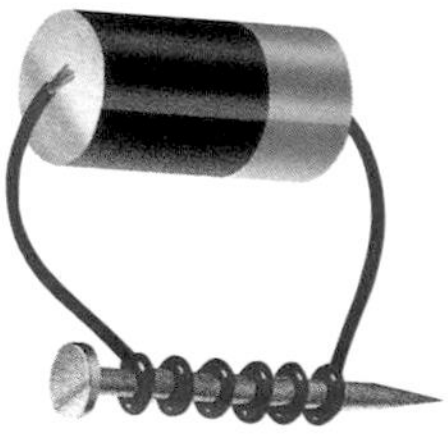

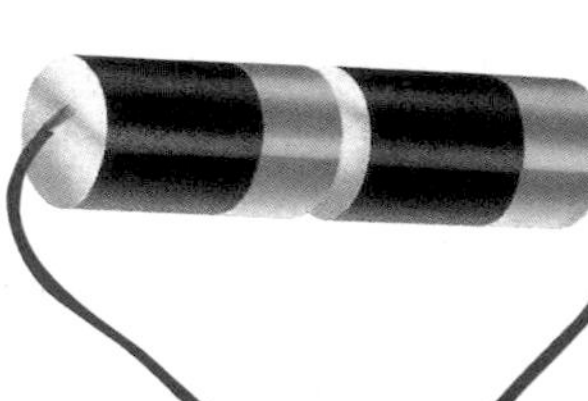

WHY IT WORKS

An electromagnet is made by coiling an insulated wire around an iron core, like an iron nail. An electric current flowing through the wire creates a magnetic field around the iron core. This causes the domains in the piece of iron to line up in the same direction, turning it into a magnet.

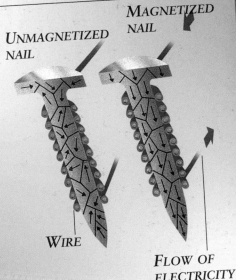

UNMAGNETIZED NAIL

MAGNETIZED NAIL

WIRE

FLOW OF ELECTRICITY

ELECTROMAGNETIC CRANE

1 Make the crane out of two boxes. Make the arm of the crane from cardboard. Attach a spool inside the arm with a pencil. Wind insulated wire around the nail at least twenty-five times. Thread both ends of the wire down the arm.

2 Attach one end of the wire to a battery terminal in the crane. Attach the other end to a thumbtack in the side of the crane. Attach a paper clip to this tack, to make a switch. Push another tack into the side of the crane and attach it to the other battery terminal by a wire.

3 When the paper clip touches both thumbtacks, the circuit is complete and the current flows. This turns the nail into an electromagnet, which can pick up metal objects.

MAGNETS AND MOTION

IN THE 1800S, WHEN ELECTROMAGNETS WERE FIRST INVENTED, people discovered that they could also make things move using electromagnetism. This is done by using a coil of wire wrapped around a tube, called a solenoid. Solenoids are used in switches, such as some doorbells. Make your own solenoid and watch the mouse duck into the cheese.

PEEKING MOUSE

1 Cut out three squares and two triangles of cardboard to make a wedge of cheese. Make a hole in one of the squares for the mouse to peek out of. Make sure one of the sides can be opened and closed.

2 Coil a piece of insulated wire around a plastic drinking straw. Place it on some modeling clay inside the cheese wedge, opposite the hole. Make a small hole in the triangular door and thread the ends of the wire through it.

WHY IT WORKS

The current running through the wire produces a magnetic field. This field is made stronger because the wire is coiled close together. The needle is attracted to the magnetic field and is pulled inside the coil.

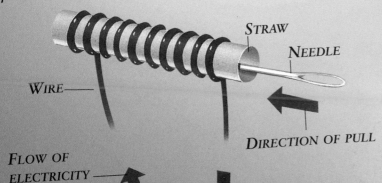

STRAW

NEEDLE

WIRE

DIRECTION OF PULL

FLOW OF ELECTRICITY

3 Make a mouse's face from paper, and attach it to the end of the needle with modeling clay. Make sure the mouse's head fits through the hole.

4 Slide the needle into the straw, leaving the mouse peeking out of the hole. Connect the wire to a battery and watch the mouse.

MAGNETS AND MOTORS

AFTER SCIENTISTS FOUND THEY COULD MAKE THINGS MOVE WITH MAGNETISM, British scientist Michael Faraday produced continuous motion by passing an electric current through a metal wire in a strong magnetic field. He developed a forerunner of the electric motor in 1821. You can produce continuous motion in this project by getting a compass needle to spin.

WHAT YOU NEED
Two batteries
Adhesive tape
Cardboard tube
Paper
Insulated wire
Compass

2 *Wrap insulated copper wire at least fifty times around a short, wide cardboard tube. Leave the two ends of the wire free to connect to the batteries.*

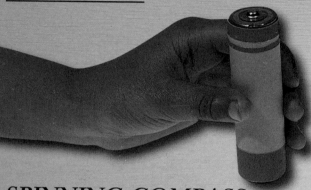

SPINNING COMPASS

1 *Place two batteries end to end so that opposite terminals are touching. Wrap them in paper to keep them together.*

3 *Attach the coil of wire to a base with adhesive tape. Attach the batteries to the base in the same way.*

WHY IT WORKS

The current turns the coil into an electromagnet and attracts the compass needle. When the current is turned on and off rapidly, the compass needle spins around. An electric motor works on this principle.

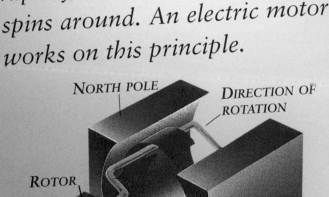

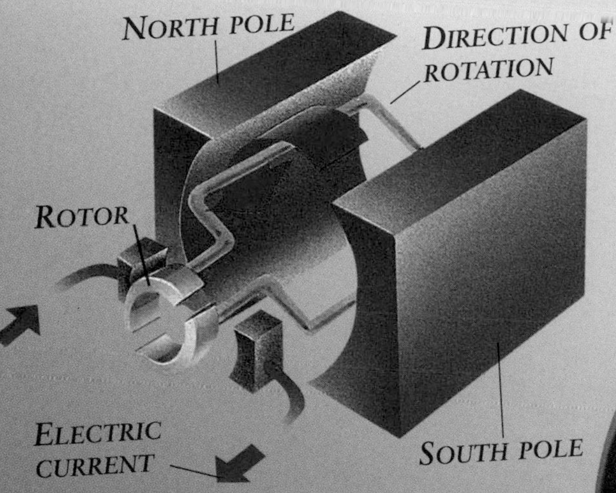

NORTH POLE

DIRECTION OF ROTATION

ROTOR

ELECTRIC CURRENT

SOUTH POLE

MAKING A CURRENT

A magnet moving near a coil of wire creates an electric current in the wire. This is called a dynamo. Where can you find dynamos? Some bicycle lights are run on a dynamo attached to the bicycle's wheels.

4 Place a compass inside the coil. Connect the wires to the ends of the batteries and see what happens to the compass needle. Now repeatedly connect and disconnect one of the wires to the battery and see what happens to the compass needle.

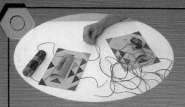

MAKING CURRENT

IN 1831, BOTH BRITISH SCIENTIST MICHAEL FARADAY and American physicist Joseph Henry discovered that moving a magnet through a coiled wire causes an electric current to flow through the wire. Soon the induction coil was developed, where a varying current flowing through one coil of wire causes a current to flow through a second coil of wire within a magnetic field. Make an induction coil for yourself.

WHAT YOU NEED
Cardboard tubes and squares
Insulated wire
Compass
Adhesive tape
Iron nail
Battery

INDUCTION COIL

1 *Wrap a length of insulated wire fifty times around a large iron nail. Secure each end with adhesive tape to keep the coil from unwinding. Leave about 4 inches free at each end of the wire so you can attach it to a battery.*

2 *Over the first coil, wrap the middle section of the second piece of wire fifty times in the opposite direction and secure with adhesive tape.*

3 *Wrap a third piece of wire about thirty times around a compass and connect its ends to the ends of the second piece of wire so that the compass can sit about 3 feet away from the coiled nail. This is to prevent the nail from directly affecting the compass.*

4 Make holders for the compass and the nail out of flattened cardboard tubes and squares of cardboard.

5 Connect one end of the first wire to a battery terminal. Touch the other end of the wire to the other battery terminal, repeatedly switching the current on and off. The compass needle will swing back and forth every time you do this.

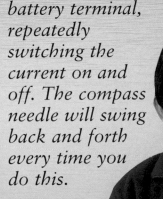

WHY IT WORKS

Because the current in the first coil is constantly interrupted, it causes its own magnetic field to change all the time. This changing magnetic field creates an electrical field in the second coil, causing a current to flow. Induction only works when the current is changing.

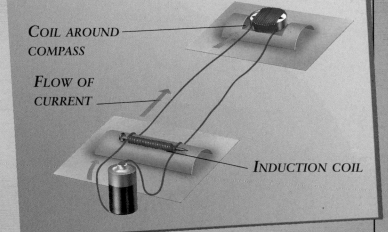

COIL AROUND COMPASS

FLOW OF CURRENT

INDUCTION COIL

VOLTAGE

Put more turns into the second coil. This increases the strength, or voltage, generated in the second coil. What happens to the compass needle?

CHAPTER 5

LIGHT & SIGHT

INTRODUCTION

Our world is filled with light and color, from the brightness of a sunny day to the many shades of a rainbow. In this chapter you will find out how we can see things and what makes us see different colors. The projects will give you a good introduction to the world of telescopes, microscopes, and cameras, as well as a chance to see how fiber-optics work.

CONTENTS

LIGHT FOR LIFE

WHAT YOU NEED
Shallow tray
Cotton balls
Sprout seeds
Cardboard

THE BRIGHTEST AND MOST OBVIOUS SOURCE OF LIGHT IS OUR NEAREST STAR, THE SUN. The sun supplies us, as well as plants and animals, with light and warmth — without it we would not be able to survive! This experiment offers an introduction to the world of light by showing you just how important sunlight is in keeping plants alive.

GROWING PLANTS

1 *Spread the cotton balls in the tray. Moisten the cotton balls with water and scatter the sprout seeds over them. Leave it until the seeds have sprouted.*

2 *Ask an adult to cut out your initials or a pattern from the cardboard. Place this over the seedlings.*

3 *Leave the tray in a sunny spot for about two weeks, keeping the cotton balls moist with water.*

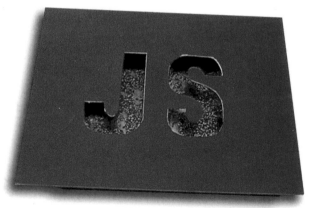

4 *When the sprouts have fully grown, remove the cardboard. You will see that the sprouts exposed to the light by your cutout initials are much greener.*

TURNING SEEDS

Plants always grow toward the light. You can see this by placing a seedling on a windowsill. After one week you will see that it has started to grow toward the light. Turn the pot around, and it will start to grow back toward the light.

WHY IT WORKS

Plants use sunlight, a gas in the air called carbon dioxide, and water to make food that they use to grow. At the same time, they release a gas called oxygen into the air. If the plants are kept in the dark, they cannot make their food, so they will wither and be paler than those exposed to the sun.

SUNLIGHT

CARBON DIOXIDE ABSORBED

WATER ABSORBED

OXYGEN RELEASED

IN CAMERA

WHAT YOU NEED
Cardboard box
Sharp pencil
Tracing paper
Paints
Adhesive tape
Blanket

LIGHT FROM THE SUN, AS WELL AS ALL OTHER FORMS OF LIGHT, travels in straight lines as light rays. As a result, light cannot naturally turn corners, which is why shadows are created (see pages 98–99). Because light only travels in straight lines, it can even appear to turn the world upside down, as this project to make your own pinhole camera reveals.

PINHOLE CAMERA

1 *Ask an adult to cut the back off a cardboard box. Decorate the box using the paints.*

2 *Ask an adult to make a small round hole in the front of the box using a sharp pencil.*

BLURRED IMAGE

Using the sharp pencil, ask an adult to make the hole in your camera slightly larger. The image on the screen will become fuzzy. This is because the larger hole lets more light rays enter the camera. These light rays then hit the screen at lots of different angles, making the picture become fuzzy.

3 Tape a sheet of tracing paper to the back of the box.

4 Pull the blanket over your head and the back of the camera. Point the camera at a bright window and you will be able to see an upside-down image of the window on the tracing paper in the back of the box.

WHY IT WORKS

The opening of the pinhole camera is very small. When rays of light from the window enter the camera, they cross over because they travel in a straight line. As a result, the image on the screen is upside down. The same thing happens with your eye. Light rays cross over as they pass through the pupil and enter the eyeball. When they hit the retina, they form an upside-down image. This image is sent to the brain, which turns the picture around again, letting you see the world the right way up!

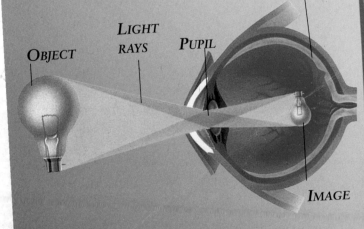

OBJECT
LIGHT RAYS
PUPIL
RETINA
IMAGE

IN THE DARK

Now that you know that light rays travel in straight lines (see pages 96–97), you can explore some of the effects of this. One of these effects is shadows. Look at your feet, and if it's a sunny day or you're in a bright room, you will see your shadow stretching off in the opposite direction from the light. This shadow is formed because your body blocks light rays and stops them from lighting up the dark area. Make your own puppet theater and have some fun experimenting with shadows.

WHAT YOU
NEED
Dark cardboard
Paper fasteners
Tracing paper
Tape, Glue
Drinking straws
Flashlight

WHY IT WORKS

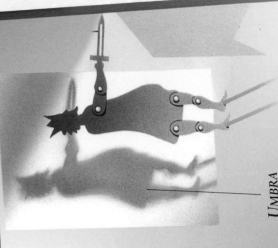

UMBRA

The dark area, or shadow, is caused by an absence of light. Rays of light from your flashlight are blocked by your puppet before they can reach the screen. This creates an area of the screen in the shape of your puppet that is darker than the rest of the screen. The completely dark part of the shadow is called the umbra.

SHADOW PUPPETS

1 Ask an adult to cut out the body parts of the puppets from the dark cardboard, as shown above.

2 Join the body parts together using the paper fasteners, making sure that the limbs can be moved.

3 Glue the straws to the feet of the puppet. These will help you to control the puppet.

4 Cut a semicircle out of a sheet of cardboard. Tape tracing paper over this hole to make the screen. Tape some cardboard supports to the back to keep the screen upright.

5 Shine the flashlight from behind the screen and entertain your friends by having your shadow puppets perform a story for them.

BLURRING SHADOWS

Move the puppets away from the screen, and their shadows become blurred, with an area of half-shadow around the edge. This half-shadow is called a penumbra.

TRANSPARENT, TRANSLUCENT, AND OPAQUE

YOU'VE ALREADY SEEN HOW LIGHT CAN BE BLOCKED BY SOME OBJECTS. Now you can see how light can actually pass through things! When light can pass through something, that object is called see-through, or transparent. However, some objects appear cloudy and only let some light through. They are called translucent. Other objects that let no light through are called opaque. This project will help you explore things that are transparent, translucent, and opaque.

WHAT YOU NEED
Glass jar
Water
Milk
Flashlight

CLOUDY WATERS

1 Fill a glass jar with water. Shine a flashlight through the water-filled jar onto a white wall or piece of paper behind it. You will see that white light from the flashlight travels all the way through the jar and the water.

SEE-THROUGH PAPER

Hold a sheet of white paper up to the light, and it appears opaque. Now soak the paper in water, hold it up, and you will see that light can pass through it. This is because the water that soaks into the paper helps light pass through the gaps between the tiny paper fibers.

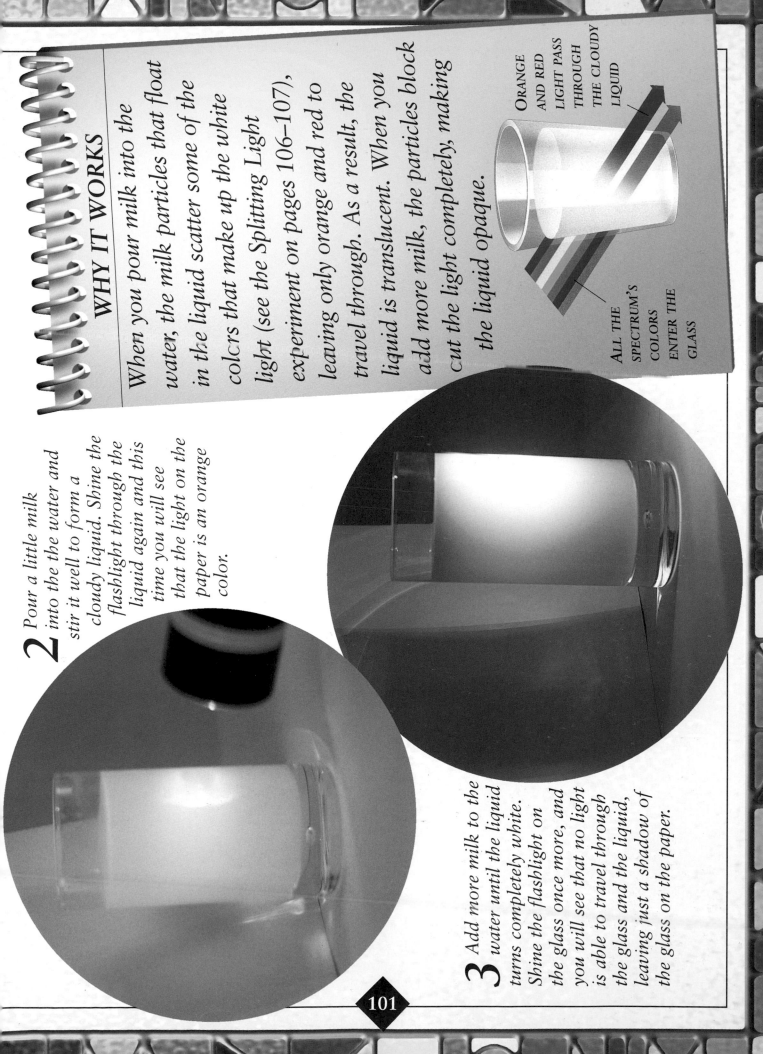

WHY IT WORKS

When you pour milk into the water, the milk particles that float in the liquid scatter some of the colors that make up the white light (see the Splitting Light light (see the Splitting Light experiment on pages 106–107), leaving only orange and red to travel through. As a result, the liquid is translucent. When you add more milk, the particles block cut the light completely, making the liquid opaque.

ORANGE AND RED LIGHT PASS THROUGH THE CLOUDY LIQUID

ALL THE SPECTRUM'S COLORS ENTER THE GLASS

2 Pour a little milk into the the water and stir it well to form a cloudy liquid. Shine the flashlight through the liquid again and this time you will see that the light on the paper is an orange color.

3 Add more milk to the water until the liquid turns completely white. Shine the flashlight on the glass once more, and you will see that no light is able to travel through the glass and the liquid, leaving just a shadow of the glass on the paper.

BENDING LIGHT

IT CAN SOMETIMES BE HELPFUL TO BEND LIGHT RAYS SLIGHTLY.

This bending is called refraction. Eyeglasses use refraction to bend rays of light, helping people to see things clearly. Microscopes also bend light rays to make objects appear bigger. Make a simple microscope in this project and see how bending light rays can be useful.

WHAT YOU NEED

Clear plastic bottle
Small, flat mirror
Modeling clay
Drop of water
Scissors

MICROSCOPE

1 Ask an adult to cut the top off a plastic bottle and then cut out a narrow strip from two opposite sides of the lower half of the bottle.

2 Ask an adult to cut two horizontal slits in the other two sides of the bottle, near the top.

3 Push the two ends of one of the plastic strips through these two slits to form a platform.

BROKEN PENCILS

Fill a glass with water and place a pencil in it. When you look at the pencil from the side it appears as if the part of the pencil in the water has become bent or broken. This is because the water refracts, or bends, light rays from the pencil, making the underwater part appear as if it is in a slightly different position.

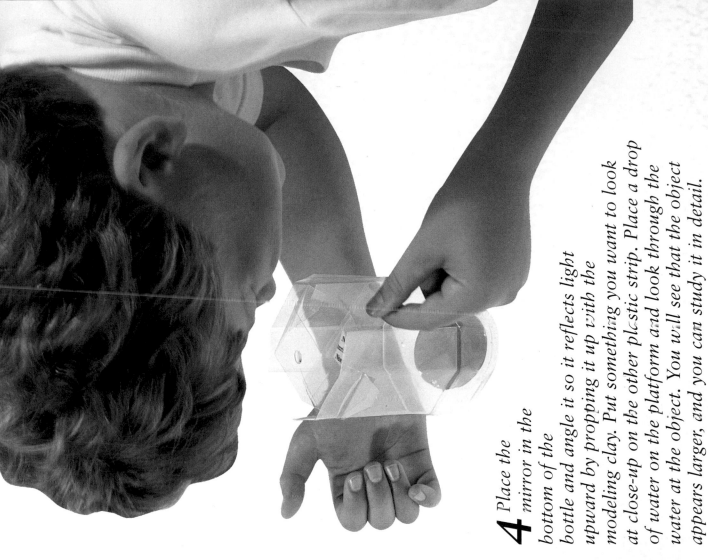

4 Place the mirror in the bottom of the bottle and angle it so it reflects light upward by propping it up with the modeling clay. Put something you want to look at close-up on the other plastic strip. Place a drop of water on the platform and look through the water at the object. You will see that the object appears larger, and you can study it in detail.

WHY IT WORKS

The drop of water on the platform acts as a small lens. When light rays from the object pass through the drop of water, they are bent, or refracted. This occurs in such a way that they make the object appear larger when you look at it.

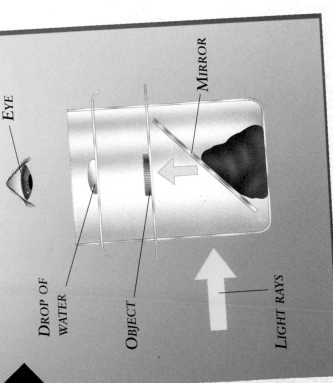

EYE

DROP OF WATER

OBJECT

MIRROR

LIGHT RAYS

103

BRINGING IT CLOSER

TELESCOPES HAVE BEEN USED FOR HUNDREDS OF YEARS to look at faraway objects. Just like the microscope you made on the previous page, many telescopes use bulging, or convex, lenses to bend, or refract, light rays. This makes objects appear closer than they actually are. Build your own telescope in this project and see how it can boost your power of vision.

LOOKING INTO THE DISTANCE

1 *Fit one of the convex lenses in one end of the wide cardboard tube.*

2 *Fit the other lens into the eyepiece.*

3 *Insert the eyepiece into one end of the narrow cardboard tube. Hold it in place using some of the modeling clay.*

WHY IT WORKS

The lens at the front of the telescope gathers light rays from far away, while the lens in the eyepiece bends these light rays again to produce a larger image. By sliding the tubes back and forth you can make objects at different distances come into focus.

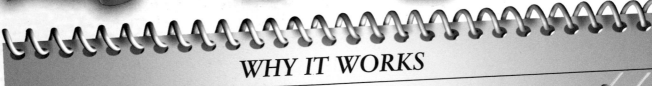

LIGHT RAYS

FOCUSING LIGHT

Hold one of the lenses in front of a flashlight and shine the light onto a wall. Now move the lens toward and away from the flashlight. You will see that the size of the light beam changes as you move the lens. You should be able to focus the light into a small dot on the wall.

4 Push the narrow tube into the wide tube, making sure they slide together smoothly.

5 Hold your telescope up to your eye and slide the tubes into and out of each other until a distant object comes into focus and appears much closer.

SPLITTING LIGHT

IN THE EXPERIMENT ON PAGES 100–101, you learned that light can come in different colors. This is because what we see as white light is actually lots of different colors mixed together. Sometimes these colors split to form a rainbow. This multicolored band of light is called a spectrum. You can split white light up into a spectrum with this simple project.

WHAT YOU NEED

Large glass bowl
Bulldog clips
Adhesive tape
Black cardboard
White cardboard
Mirror
Scissors

SPLITTING WHITE LIGHT

1 Seal the edges of the mirror with the adhesive tape.

2 Ask an adult to cut a narrow slit in the middle of the black cardboard.

WHY IT WORKS

The angled mirror creates a triangular-shaped region near the surface of the water. This shape is called a prism. As sunlight travels through the prism, the light is split up to form a spectrum. Raindrops act as tiny prisms, splitting sunlight to create rainbows.

WHITE LIGHT HITS WATER

WHITE LIGHT SPLIT INTO A SPECTRUM BY THE WATER

3 Half-fill the glass bowl with water.

4 Using the bulldog clips, fix the mirror in the bowl of water so that it rests at an angle.

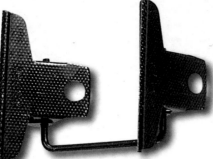

5 Point the mirror at a bright window and place the black cardboard in front of it. Now place the white cardboard below the slit and adjust the mirror until you see a spectrum appear on the piece of white cardboard.

COMPACT COLORS

Look at the playing surface of a compact disc. The tiny notches etched onto the surface split light up, creating a spectrum that you will be able to see as you view the compact disc from different angles.

MIXING LIGHT

WHAT YOU NEED
Three flashlights
Red, blue, and
green cellophane
Three cardboard
tubes
Adhesive tape
White cardboard

JUST AS YOU CAN SPLIT LIGHT INTO DIFFERENT COLORS (see pages 106–107), so you can mix colored lights together. Televisions use this principle to make color pictures. Look very closely at your television screen (not for too long, though!), and you will see that it is made up of thousands of tiny blue, red, and green dots. This project shows how you can mix colored lights to form new colors.

COLOR WHEELS

Color a circle of white cardboard with the colors of the spectrum in different segments. Ask an adult to push a sharp pencil through the middle. Then spin the wheel as fast as you can. The colors on the wheel will appear to blur and mix, making the wheel look white.

COLORED SPOTS

1 *Cut out squares of the red, blue, and green cellophane that are big enough to fit over the ends of the cardboard tubes.*

2 *Fix the cellophane squares to the ends of the tubes using the adhesive tape.*

WHY IT WORKS

The new colors are made by mixing the three colored lights on the white background. For example, red and green will form yellow. If you mixed all three colors together, they would form white light!

3 Place a sheet of white cardboard on the floor in a darkened room. With a couple of friends, hold the tubes and shine the flashlights down them onto the white cardboard.

4 Now move the spots of colored light so that they overlap and create new colors of light on the cardboard.

SEPARATING COLORS

MIXING COLORED LIGHTS (SEE PAGES 108–109) is not the only way to create new colors. Just like the colors on a television screen, the colors on this page are made up from tiny dots. This time the colors of these dots are magenta (pink), cyan (blue), yellow, and black. These colors, called pigments, are mixed together in different quantities to create all the other colors.

SPLITTING PIGMENTS

1 Cut the blotting paper into strips and draw patterns on them using a different colored pen for each strip.

2 Place the strips in the bowl so that only their bottoms are in the water while the rest hangs over the side.

3 Watch as the water soaks into the strips of blotting paper and starts to separate the ink into its different colored ingredients, or pigments.

4 When the water has completely soaked the strips of blotting paper, take them out and closely examine the strips to see which pigments make up each color.

INKY RINGS

Cut out a circle of blotting paper. Draw a large spot in the middle, using a water-based pen.

Then cut a strip from the spot in the center to the edge and fold it down so that it hangs in the water.

As the water soaks into the paper, the color will separate, forming circles of pigments.

WHY IT WORKS

As the water soaks into the strips of blotting paper, it carries the pigments with it because they are water soluble (they can mix with water). However, the different pigments that make up the colors are carried by the water at different rates. As a result, the pigments are separated into bands, allowing you to see which pigments make up the colors. For example, red ink is made up of yellow and magenta pigments.

BEAMS OF LIGHT

LIGHT CAN BE USED TO CARRY LOTS OF INFORMATION along miles and miles of special glass wires called fiber-optic cables. These beams of light can carry sound and pictures, such as telephone conversations and television pictures. This experiment shows you how these cables can carry light rays over the most winding routes, despite the fact that light travels in a straight line.

WHAT YOU
NEED
Black paint
Flashlight
Pin
*Large glass
bowl*
*Clear plastic
bottle*

FIBER OPTICS

1 *Ask an adult to cut the top off the plastic bottle. Paint the outside of the bottle black, leaving a small area clear on one side. Using the pin, make a small hole in the bottle on the opposite side from the clear area.*

WHY IT WORKS

The stream of water acts like a fiber-optic wire. As the rays of light travel down the stream, they bounce, or reflect, off the sides, traveling along the stream even as it bends. The rays of light hit the stream's sides at such a shallow angle that they are reflected inside. In the same way, fiber-optic cables

112

carry light rays along a curved path by reflecting them off the sides of the fibers.

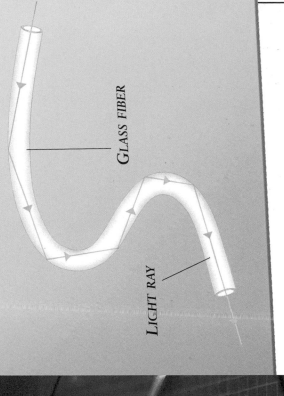

GLASS FIBER

LIGHT RAY

REMOTE CONTROL

Your TV remote control uses invisible beams of light to change channels. Try covering the front of the remote control with your hand. You will find that the remote control will not work because your hand blocks the light.

2 In a darkened room, stand the bottle against one side of the bowl so that the clear area faces out. Fill the bottle with water and shine the flashlight through the clear area. Place your finger in the stream of water and you should be able to see a spot of light.

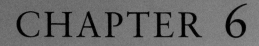

CHAPTER 6

SOUND & MUSIC

INTRODUCTION

You can hear sounds all the time, from the rustle of leaves in a tree to the pounding beat of a rock concert. Sound can be bounced or reflected off solid objects. It can also be produced by making objects vibrate. Read on and find out how sounds are made and how we hear them. Try the projects and learn more about echoes and vibrations, telephones, and musical instruments.

CONTENTS

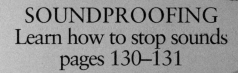

115

RIPPLES IN THE AIR

YOU CAN HEAR SOUNDS AROUND YOU ALL THE TIME. Whether they are the roar of a jet plane taking off or the faint rustle of leaves in a tree, sounds are always reaching your ears. But what arc these sounds, how are they caused, and how is it that they can travel from their source to you? This first experiment looks at how sounds are made and also explains how they travel through the air and reach your ears.

WATER WAVES

The next time you are near a pond or lake, carefully drop a small stone into the water. When the stone hits the water, it creates a disturbance that forms ripples on the surface. These ripples quickly spread out away from the source of the disturbance in much the same way that sound waves travel through the air.

DRUM BEATS

1 Stretch the plastic wrap over the top of the waste basket and hold it in place with the rubber bands.

2 Wrap the basket with a rectangle of white cardboard that is big enough to go around it. Decorate this with pieces of colored cardboard.

3 Paint the ends of the wooden sticks to make your drumsticks.

WHY IT WORKS

When you beat the skin of your drum, it starts to vibrate. As the skin vibrates, it causes the air around it to shake, creating a series of waves of sound. These sound waves spread out from the drum like ripples on a pond. When these waves reach you, your ears change these waves into sounds that you hear.

SOUND WAVES

4 Beat the plastic skin of your drum to make a noise.

117

THE POWER OF SOUND

see pages 116-117

WHAT YOU NEED
*Colored
cardboard
Paper plates
Empty spools
Wooden stick
Plastic wrap
Adhesive tape
Tissue paper
Drinking straw*

ALTHOUGH SOUND WAVES SPREAD OUT LIKE THE RIPPLES ON A POND (see pages 116-117), you cannot see them. They are invisible as they travel through the air. However, you can sometimes feel their effects, especially if they are loud and strong enough. Build your own sound cannon in this project and see just how powerful these sound waves can be.

SOUND CANNON

1 *Make a pair of wheels for your sound cannon by sticking two paper plates onto two circles of cardboard. Stick the spools to the inside of each wheel and then push the stick into the other side of the spools to make the axle.*

3 *Cut out a circle of cardboard big enough to cover the front of your cannon. This circle should have a small hole cut out of its middle.*

4 *Tape it onto the front of your cannon.*

5 *Set your cannon onto the wheels and weight the back end down so the cannon won't tip over. Now make a curtain by gluing tissue paper strips to a straw.*

2 *Make a wide tube from a large sheet of cardboard. Stretch plastic wrap over a ring of cardboard and tape it to one end of the tube. This will be the back of your cannon.*

6 *Aim the cannon at the tissue paper curtain and tap the plastic wrap quite hard. You should see the strips of tissue paper move as you make the noises.*

MOVING AWAY

Move the cannon away from the curtain and find out your cannon's range when the strips stop moving.

WHY IT WORKS

When you tap the plastic wrap, it creates sound waves inside the cannon. Because of the small hole at the front of the cannon, these sound waves come out of the cannon in a narrow beam. As these sound waves hit the curtain, they cause the strips of tissue paper to move, letting you see the power of sound.

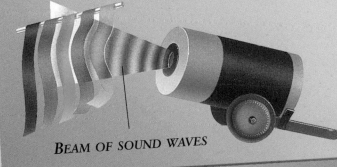

BEAM OF SOUND WAVES

KNOCKING IT OVER

Cut some shapes out of paper and prop them up by folding the base of each shape over at a right angle. Now aim your sound cannon at the shapes and see if the sound waves from it are powerful enough to knock them over.

BOUNCING SOUNDS

FROM THE PREVIOUS EXPERIMENTS, you have seen that sounds spread out from their source in waves (see pages 116–117) and that these waves have the power to move things and cause them to vibrate (see pages 118–119).

However, what happens to sounds when they come across a surface that is harder than a tissue paper curtain? This experiment shows you that, just like rays of light bouncing off a shiny surface or mirror, sound waves can bounce around to form echoes.

WHAT YOU NEED
Colored paper
Stiff cardboard
Ticking clock

SOUND REFLECTIONS

1 Find a continuous sound source, such as a ticking clock. Prop up the piece of stiff cardboard to make your sound wall.

2 Roll the colored paper into two tubes. They will be your listening tubes. Place them in a V shape against the sound wall.

WHY IT WORKS

The sounds made by the ticking clock are channeled down one cardboard tube. They reflect off the sound wall along the other cardboard tube, where you hear the sound reflection, or echo.

120

This will only work if the sound wall is hard. If it is soft, then it will absorb the sound waves, and no sound will be reflected.

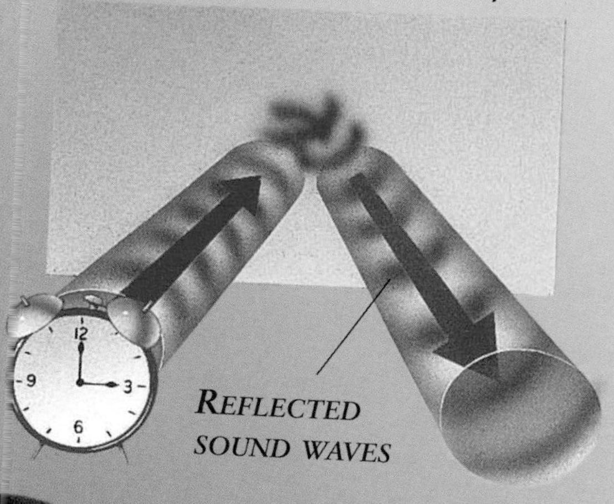

REFLECTED
SOUND WAVES

CHANGING THE ANGLE

Move your listening tube around. You will find that the volume of the ticking changes. That's because the sound waves from the clock are reflected at a certain angle. Away from this angle, the listening tube picks up fewer sound waves and the volume is lower.

3 Place the ticking clock at the open end of one of the tubes and listen at the other. You will hear that the sound of the ticking clock appears to be coming along the paper tube.

121

COLLECTING SOUNDS

YOU NOW KNOW THAT SOUNDS WAVES bounce around you all the time, but do you know how they get inside your head? On either side of your head are two special sound-collecting devices — your ears! Take a close look at a friend's ears. You'll see that the outer ears are shaped like flattened funnels — this is no accident. You can see how funnels help improve your hearing with this experiment.

WHAT YOU NEED
*Colored
cardboard
Adhesive tape
Pencil
String*

LOUD AND QUIET

Now turn the ear trumpet the other way around and you'll find that sounds become quieter. This is because very few sound waves can enter the trumpet through its smaller hole. Any that do quickly lose their energy in the trumpet without reaching your ear. You can also use your ear trumpet as a megaphone to make your voice louder.

4 Hold the ear trumpet to your ear and listen as it makes sounds louder.

EAR TRUMPET

1 Draw a large semicircle on the colored cardboard using some string and a pencil. Ask an adult to cut this semicircle out to form the template for your ear trumpet.

2 Roll the semicircle of cardboard and stick it together so that it forms a cone that is open at both ends.

3 Fasten a strip of cardboard to the side of the cone to act as the handle for your ear trumpet. Decorate your ear trumpet.

WHY IT WORKS

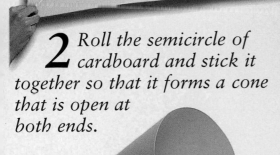

The ear trumpet collects sound waves and keeps them from escaping into the surrounding air. The energy of these sound waves is then channeled into your ear. Because more sound energy reaches your ear, the sounds you hear seem louder.

HEARING SOUNDS

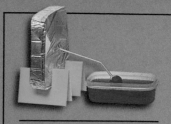

THE "COLLECTING SOUNDS" EXPERIMENT (SEE PAGES 122–123) showed you how the funnels that form your outer ears collect sounds and channel them into your brain.
But how does the ear change these sound waves into signals that your brain can understand? Build your own artificial ear and see how your complicated inner ear works.

WHAT YOU NEED
Colored cardboard
Flexible drinking straw
Ping-Pong ball
Foil tray
Plastic wrap
Glue
Adhesive tape
Bowl of water

BUILDING AN EAR

1 Make a cardboard base for your artificial ear, big enough to support the foil tray.

2 Cut a hole from the bottom of the foil tray. Ask an adult to do this for you since the edges can be sharp.

3 Stretch plastic wrap over the top of the foil tray.

WHY IT WORKS

Just as the sound waves from your sound cannon made the tissue curtain vibrate (see pages 118-119), the sound waves from your voice make the plastic wrap vibrate. This vibrates the straw, causing ripples in the water. Inside your ear is a film called the eardrum. This vibrates when sound waves hit it, causing three tiny bones to vibrate. These create ripples in the fluid inside an organ called the cochlea. These ripples are turned into signals that are then sent to the brain.

EARDRUM
EAR BONES
COCHLEA

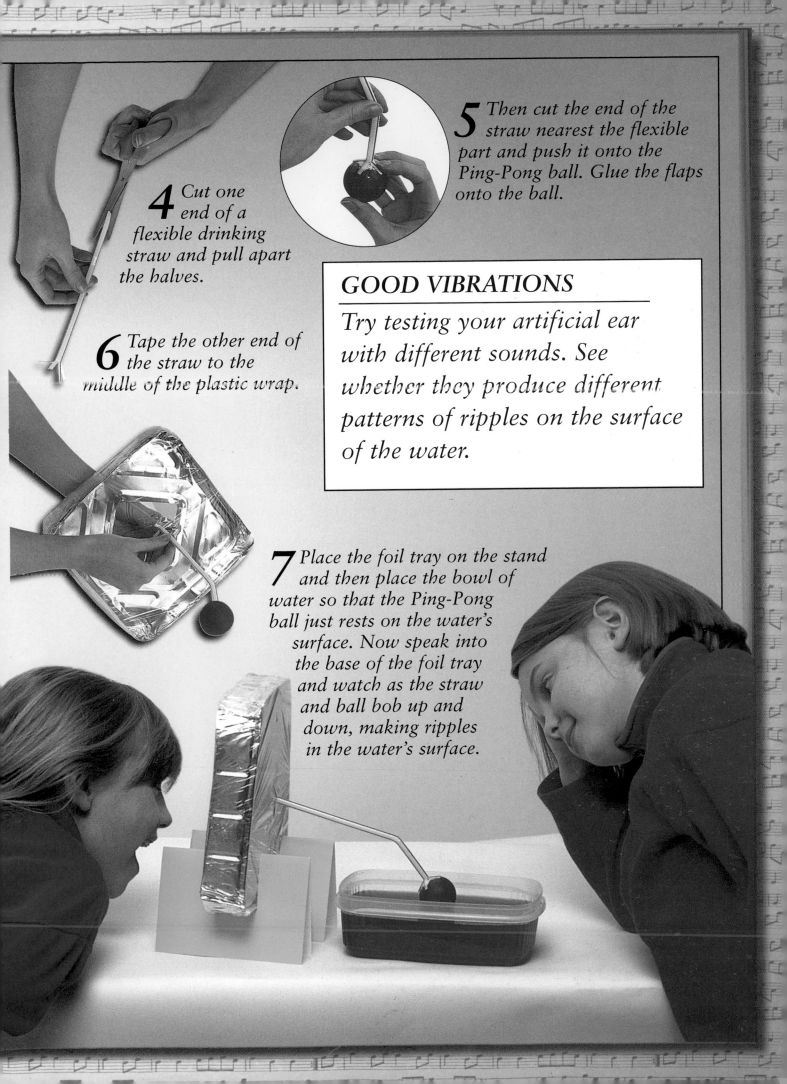

4 Cut one end of a flexible drinking straw and pull apart the halves.

5 Then cut the end of the straw nearest the flexible part and push it onto the Ping-Pong ball. Glue the flaps onto the ball.

6 Tape the other end of the straw to the middle of the plastic wrap.

GOOD VIBRATIONS

Try testing your artificial ear with different sounds. See whether they produce different patterns of ripples on the surface of the water.

7 Place the foil tray on the stand and then place the bowl of water so that the Ping-Pong ball just rests on the water's surface. Now speak into the base of the foil tray and watch as the straw and ball bob up and down, making ripples in the water's surface.

STEREO SOUNDS

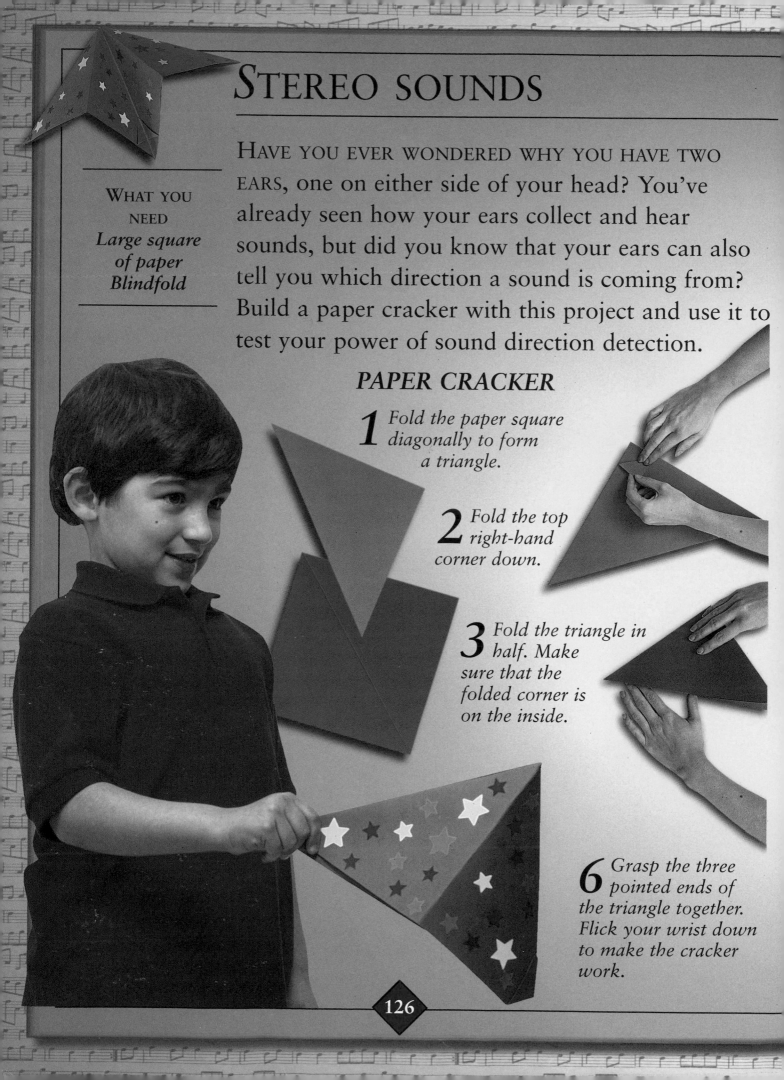

WHAT YOU NEED
Large square of paper
Blindfold

HAVE YOU EVER WONDERED WHY YOU HAVE TWO EARS, one on either side of your head? You've already seen how your ears collect and hear sounds, but did you know that your ears can also tell you which direction a sound is coming from? Build a paper cracker with this project and use it to test your power of sound direction detection.

PAPER CRACKER

1 Fold the paper square diagonally to form a triangle.

2 Fold the top right-hand corner down.

3 Fold the triangle in half. Make sure that the folded corner is on the inside.

6 Grasp the three pointed ends of the triangle together. Flick your wrist down to make the cracker work.

WHY IT WORKS

Because your ears are on the sides of your head, sounds from one side arrive at each ear at slightly different times. The sound will reach the nearest ear before the one on the far side of your head. Even though the time difference is less than one-hundredth of a second, your brain can spot the difference and figure out which direction the sound came from.

4 *Make a crease down the middle, but don't fold it.*

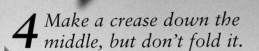

5 *From the open end of the triangle, fold the top layer of paper over along the crease. Flip the triangle over and repeat. Now decorate your cracker with bright colors.*

7 *Sit in the middle of a room and blindfold yourself. Now ask a friend to make noises with the cracker from different parts of the room. See if you can guess where your friend is standing each time.*

MONO HEARING

Now try the experiment again, but this time cover one of your ears. You will find it much harder to tell which direction the sounds are coming from.

THE SPEED OF SOUND

FROM ALL THE PREVIOUS EXPERIMENTS, it may seem as though sounds reach your ears the very instant they are made. However, this is not the case. Sound waves take time to travel from one spot to thc other — you might actually see something happen before you hear it! The experiments on this page let you see just how slow sound waves can be!

WHAT YOU NEED
Plastic bottle
Balloon
Rubber band
Flour
Pin

EXPLODING FLOUR

1 Ask an adult to cut the top off a plastic bottle.

2 Fix the balloon over the spout and hold it in place with a rubber band.

3 Using the bottle top as a funnel, pour some flour into the balloon.

4 Take the balloon off the funnel, inflate the balloon with air, and tie the end securely.

TIMING ECHOES

Echoes are reflections of sound off surfaces (see pages 120–121). Stand in a large building, clap your hands, and see if you can time how long the echoes last as they bounce off the walls.

WHY IT WORKS

Sound waves travel through the air a lot slower than light rays. In fact, light can travel 186,000 miles (300,000 km) in just one second! In the same amount of time, sound can travel through the air just 1,090 feet (333 meters)! In other words, light rays travel about one million times faster than sound waves. So you will see the balloon burst before you hear it.

5 Ask a friend to stand with the balloon a fairly long distance away.

6 Now get your friend to burst the balloon using the pin. You should see the cloud of flour erupt from the balloon before the bang of the bursting balloon reaches your ears.

TIMING LIGHTNING

Time the difference between seeing a flash of lightning and hearing thunder. Divide the time by five and you will have the distance of the storm in miles.

SOUNDPROOFING

WHAT YOU NEED
Egg cartons
Paints
Large cardboard box
Old towels or dust cloths
Alarm clock

YOU HAVE ALREADY SEEN HOW SOUNDS CAN BOUNCE OFF SURFACES and how some things can amplify sounds, or make them louder. But can anything make a sound quieter, or even get rid of it all together? Blocking out sound is called soundproofing, and it can sometimes be important. Ear protectors keep loud sounds from damaging ears when people work with noisy machinery. Build your own soundproof box in this project and see just how sounds can be stopped.

STOPPING SOUND

1 Decorate the egg cartons using the paints.

2 Line the four walls and the floor of the cardboard box with the towels or dust cloths.

3 Cut the egg cartons the same size as the walls and the floor of the box and place them on top of the towels, saving one for the top.

WHY IT WORKS

The bumpy walls of the egg cartons actually break up the sound waves as they bounce around the box, making them weaker and quieter. Also, the layers of towels absorb a lot of the sound, stopping it from passing to the box walls.

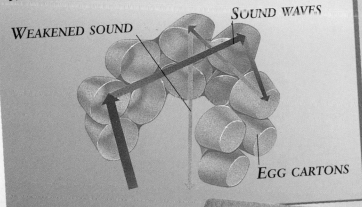

WEAKENED SOUND   SOUND WAVES

EGG CARTONS

OTHER MATERIALS

Try lining the walls of the cardboard box with other materials, such as crumpled newspaper or metal trays. Which work best to quiet the noise? You may even find that some of the materials will actually make the sound louder!

4 Set the alarm clock to go off in five minutes. Place it inside the box. Cover it with the last egg carton and another towel or dust cloth.

5 Close the box and listen to see if you can hear the alarm clock when it goes off. It will sound much quieter than normal, if you can hear it at all!

LOUD AND SOFT

THE LOUDNESS OF A SOUND is called its volume — the previous experiment showed you how to decrease the volume of a sound by soundproofing a box. But what actually determines the volume of a sound? Why, for example, is the roar of a jet plane much louder than the rustle of leaves in a tree? This experiment will show you how noises are made loud or soft.

WHAT YOU NEED

Wooden pole
String
Thumbtack
Large cardboard box
Paints
Stick

PLUCK THAT BASS

1 Decorate the long wooden pole using the paints.

2 Tie a knot in one end of the string and attach this knotted end to the top of the pole using the thumbtack.

STUFFING SOUND

The large box actually makes the sound of the string louder. It is called a resonating chamber. Place a blanket or cloth either over the hole or into the box itself. You will find that the sounds your double bass makes are quieter. This is because the cloth absorbs some of the sound energy.

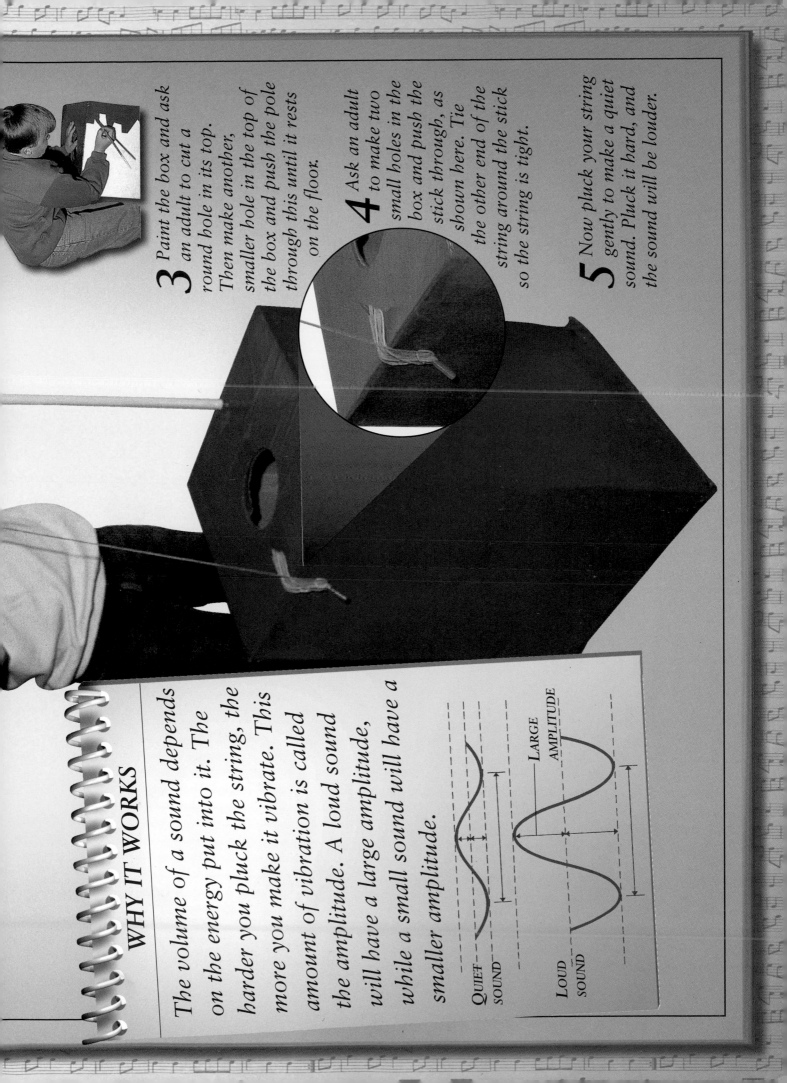

WHY IT WORKS

The volume of a sound depends on the energy put into it. The harder you pluck the string, the more you make it vibrate. This amount of vibration is called the amplitude. A loud sound will have a large amplitude, while a small sound will have a smaller amplitude.

QUIET
SOUND

LARGE
AMPLITUDE

LOUD
SOUND

3 Paint the box and ask an adult to cut a round hole in its top. Then make another, smaller hole in the top of the box and push the pole through this until it rests on the floor.

4 Ask an adult to make two small holes in the box and push the stick through, as shown here. Tie the other end of the string around the stick so the string is tight.

5 Now pluck your string gently to make a quiet sound. Pluck it hard, and the sound will be louder.

HIGH AND LOW

NOT ONLY DO SOUNDS COME IN DIFFERENT VOLUMES, they can also be high or low. Pitch is how high or low a sound or musical note is. The pitch of a note depends upon how fast a sound wave vibrates. The speed of these vibrations is called the frequency. Fast-vibrating sounds have a high pitch, while slow-vibrating sounds have a low pitch. Build your own bottle xylophone with notes of different pitches.

WHAT YOU NEED
*Five similar glass bottles
Pitcher of water
Food coloring*

BOTTLE XYLOPHONE

1 Mix some food coloring into a pitcher of water. Then pour different amounts of the colored water into the five bottles.

2 Place the bottles on a flat surface. Then tap them with a spoon and you will find that each of the bottles has a different pitch. You can alter the water level in the bottles to change their pitch so you can play a tune.

WHY IT WORKS

When each bottle is hit, the column of air above the water level starts to vibrate, creating a sound.

SLOW-VIBRATING SOUND WAVE GIVES A LOW NOTE

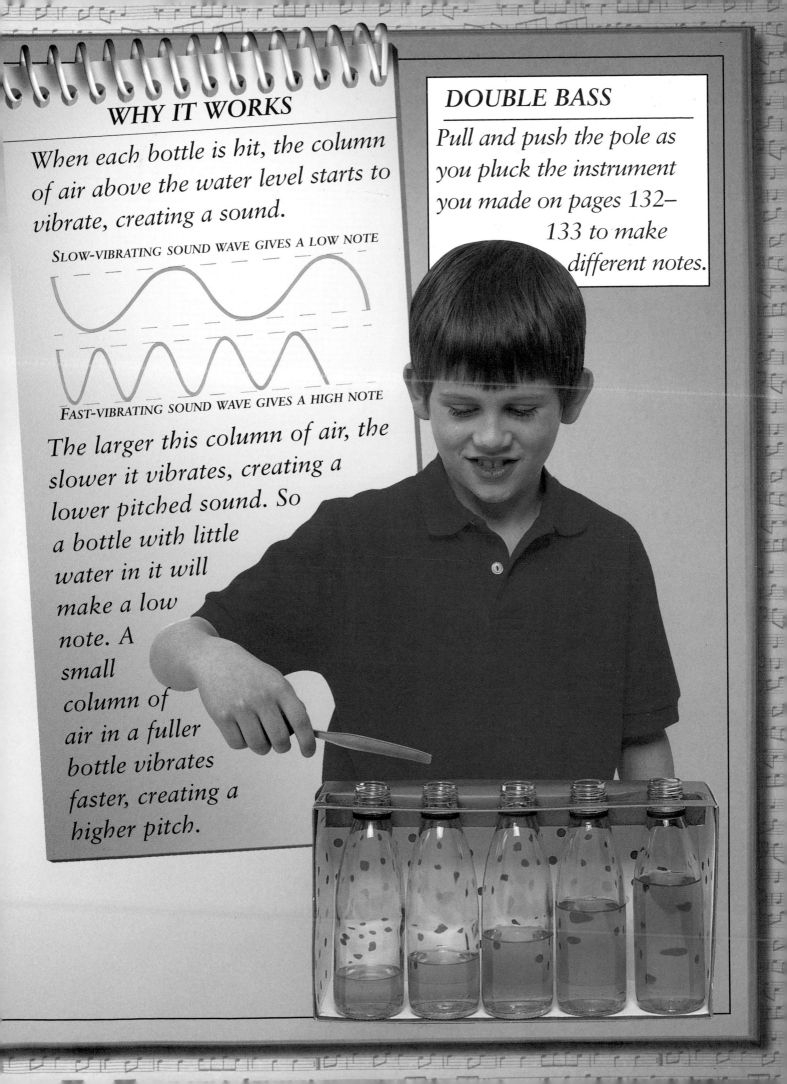

FAST-VIBRATING SOUND WAVE GIVES A HIGH NOTE

The larger this column of air, the slower it vibrates, creating a lower pitched sound. So a bottle with little water in it will make a low note. A small column of air in a fuller bottle vibrates faster, creating a higher pitch.

DOUBLE BASS

Pull and push the pole as you pluck the instrument you made on pages 132–133 to make different notes.

CHAPTER 7

UNITS & MEASUREMENTS

INTRODUCTION

Everything we do, everything we see, and everywhere we go can be measured in one kind of unit of another. Measuring in units lets you compare one distance with another, and helps you work out how far away or how heavy an object is. It also tells you how long it takes you to do something. You can even measure the wind! Read on and discover a host of experiments to teach you more about units and measurements.

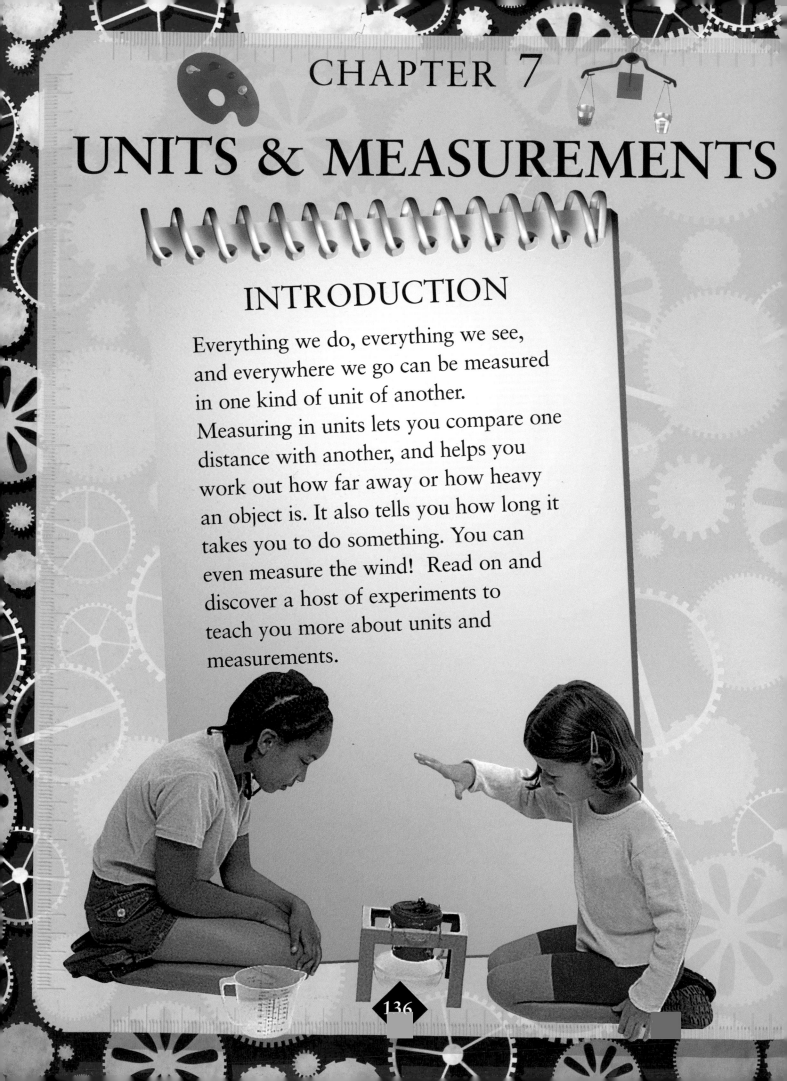

CONTENTS

HOW FAR?

HOW FAR DO YOU HAVE TO TRAVEL to school each day? How long is your bedroom? How far away is your favorite store? All of these questions are about distance. To measure distance, we use units such as inches, feet, and even miles. Build a measuring wheel in this project and see how you can measure the distance between objects.

WHAT YOU NEED
Ruler
String
Thumbtack
Pencil
Colored
cardboard
Nail
Wooden stick
Cork, Tape
Glue

SMALLER WHEEL

Use string just under 3 inches long to make another circle 18 inches around its edge. This gives a more exact reading than your first wheel, because smaller units are more accurate.

5 *To measure the distance between two objects, start with your wheel next to the first object, with the arrow pointing to the ground. Roll it to the second object in a straight line. Count how many times the arrow touches the ground before you reach the second object — this will give you the distance between the objects in yards.*

MEASURING WHEEL

1 Cut a piece of string just under 6 inches long. Tie the pencil to one end and pin the other end onto the middle of the piece of cardboard. Then draw a circle using the pencil. Ask an adult to cut the circle out.

2 Cut out an arrow shape and glue it to your circle. Point the tip of the arrow toward the edge of the circle, and the base toward the center of the circle (where the thumbtack was).

3 Tape the nail across one end of the stick, as shown. Wrap more tape around the stick to hold the first piece of tape in place.

4 Push the nail through the center of the circle. Push the cork onto the nail. Make sure the wheel can still turn.

WHY IT WORKS

Making the radius of the circle (the distance from the center to the edge) just under 6 inches makes the distance around the edge about 1 yard. The wheel goes around once for every yard covered. So the number of times it goes around equals the number of yards between the objects.

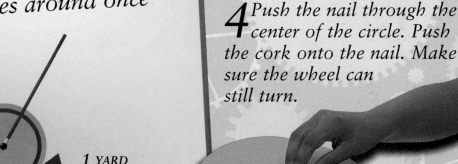

1 YARD

FINDING THE ANGLE

WHEN MAPPING OUT A PIECE OF LAND, surveyors not only need to find out the distance between points, but also the steepness of any slope, called the gradient. You may have seen surveyors at work using an instrument on a tripod called a theodolite. This tells them the angle, up or down, from where they are standing to another piece of ground. Make a simple theodolite in this project.

WHAT YOU NEED
Colored cardboard
Glue, Scissors
Pencil, Ruler
Protractor
Battery
String, Tape
Thumbtack

MEASURING HEIGHT

Surveyors also use theodolites to calculate the height of objects. By finding out the angle to the top of an object and the distance to the object from where they are standing, surveyors use simple mathematics to find out the object's height.

4 *To measure the angle between where you are and another object, simply look at the object through the two viewers. Ask somebody to read off the angle between the string and the center 0° line of the theodolite. This is the angle between you and the object.*

THEODOLITE

1 Using the method shown on page 139, draw and cut out a circle of cardboard. Cut it in half. Using the protractor and ruler, mark lines at 10° intervals. Number the lines, from 0° in the middle to 90° at either end of the flat edge.

90° — — 90°

0°

2 Make two viewers by rolling two narrow strips of cardboard into loops. Sandwich these loops between the two semicircles of cardboard and glue them all together.

3 Ask an adult to help you cover the battery with cardboard, as shown. Tape the battery to a piece of string 24 inches long to make a plumb line. Tape the other end of the string to the center of the flat edge of the semicircle. You have now made a theodolite.

WHY IT WORKS

As you raise or lower the flat edge to line it up with an object, the plumb line swings to an angle away from the 0° line. This angle is the same as the angle between yourself and the object.

0°

25°

GRID LOCK

ANOTHER MEASUREMENT surveyors often need is the amount of land something covers. This is called the area of an object. Area can be measured in a wide range of units, including acres, square inches, square feet, square yards, and square miles. Some areas are easy to find. For a square, you simply multiply the length of one side by itself. This project shows you how to find the area of simple and complicated shapes.

WHAT YOU NEED
Sheet of plastic film, Ruler Felt-tip pen Colored cardboard Scissors

SMALLER GRID

Make a grid with squares that are only $1/4$ in. across and use it to measure the area of shapes. You will find that you can measure the areas more exactly than with the larger-sized grid.

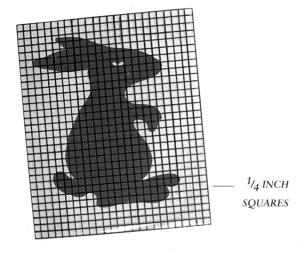

— $1/4$ INCH SQUARES

FINDING THE AREA

1 *Ask an adult to cut out different shapes from colored cardboard. Cut out simple shapes, such as squares and rectangles, and more complex ones, such as circles or animal shapes.*

2 *Using the ruler and the felt-tip pen, measure half-inch intervals along the edges of the plastic film. Join opposite points on the edges to form a grid of squares, each $1/2$ inch by $1/2$ inch.*

WHY IT WORKS

By breaking a shape up into squares, you can see the area it covers. If you ignore the less-than-half-covered squares, you can count each more-than-half-covered square as one full square. Test this by drawing a rectangle and placing the grid over it. Count the squares, then move the grid slightly. Count again, using the rule for partially covered squares. You will get the same result both times.

3 Put the grid over a shape and count the number of whole grid squares that cover the shape.

4 Now count the squares that are more than half covered, and add that to the whole squares. This gives you the area of your shape in square inches.

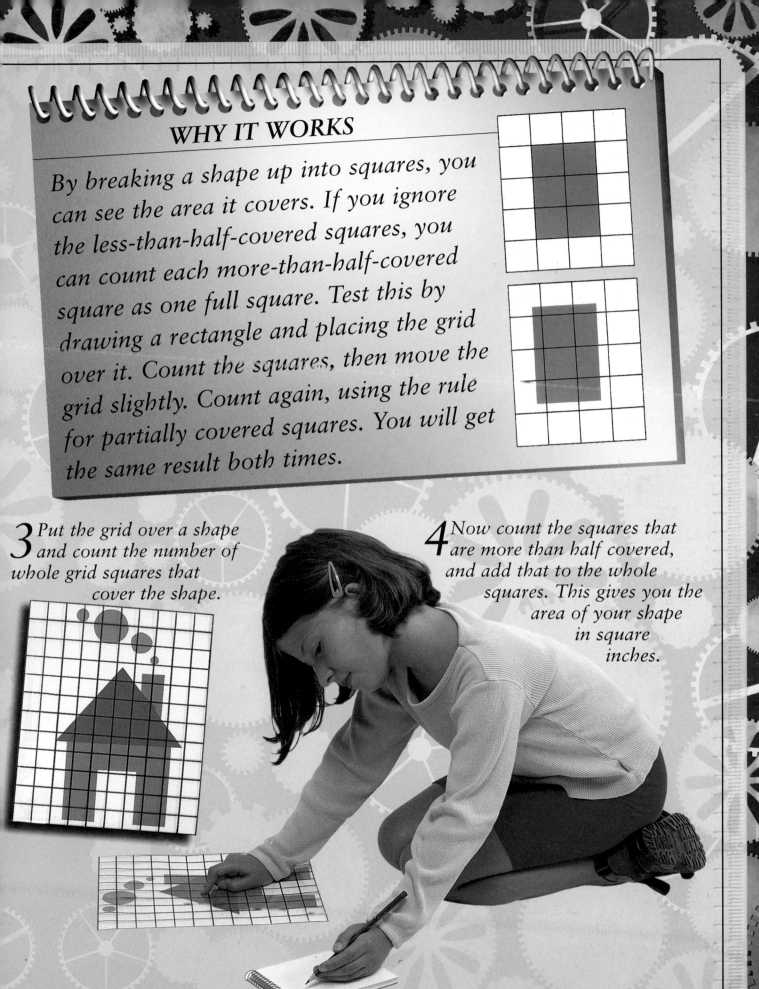

SPILLING OVER

WITH DISTANCE AND AREA, you have measured units in one and two dimensions. The amount of space an object takes up in three dimensions is called its volume. As with area, you can use simple math formulae to work out the volume of some objects — the volume of a box can be found by multiplying its base by its height by its depth. This project shows how to find the volume of any object.

WHAT YOU NEED
Cardboard box
Scissors, Glue
Colored cardboard
Two wooden sticks
Small container
Large bowl
Water
Measuring jug
Small objects

FINDING THE VOLUME

1 To make a stand, ask an adult to cut out the sides of a cardboard box. The box must be wide enough to slide the large bowl in and out.

2 To decorate the stand, cut out strips of colored cardboard. Glue the strips to the sides and top of the stand.

3 Place the sticks over your stand and balance the small container on them. Place the large bowl underneath. Fill the small container to the brim with water. Be careful not to spill water into the large bowl.

IN THE BATH

With a water-based marker, mark the level of a bath before you get in. As you get in, the level rises. Like the object in the container, your body displaces an amount of water equal to its volume.

4 Gently place an object into the small container.

5 Watch as the water spills over into the large bowl.

6 Pour the water in the large bowl into a measuring jug.

7 Put the jug on a flat surface and read off how much water is in it. This is the volume of the object you put in the container.

WHY IT WORKS

When you place the object into the small container of water, it pushes out, or displaces, a volume of water that equals its own volume. You can then measure this volume of water by pouring it into a measuring jug.

OBJECT

WATER DISPLACED BY OBJECT

LIGHT AND HEAVY

WHAT YOU NEED
Ruler
Felt-tip pen
Stiff cardboard
Plastic bottle
Paints
Scissors
Cotton thread
Piece of wood
Rubber band
Toothpick
Two nails

YOU MAY HAVE SEEN HOW ASTRONAUTS in space float around their spacecraft. They have no weight because they are so far from the earth, and moving so fast, that they are not affected by its gravity. On the earth's surface, we feel weight because weight is the combination of an object's density and the effect of the earth's gravity. This project shows you how to compare the weight of different objects.

WEIGHING IT UP

1 Use the ruler and felt-tip pen to mark out a scale along one edge of a strip of cardboard.

2 Ask an adult to cut the bottom off the plastic bottle to make a basket. Paint the basket. Ask an adult to pierce two holes near the top of the basket. Tie the thread through these holes.

3 Decorate the top of the plastic bottle using the paint. Ask an adult to cut a small flap into its base. This flap will hold the top of the bottle in place against the piece of wood.

4 Tie the rubber band to the thread on the basket. Loop the other end of the rubber band over the neck of the bottle. Attach the toothpick to the base of the basket to act as a pointer.

5 Put the piece of wood in an upright position and place the strip of cardboard against it. Ask an adult to secure the top of the bottle to the top of the piece of wood by knocking the two nails through the flap. Mark on the scale where the toothpick rests when the basket is empty.

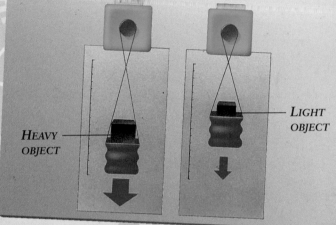

WHY IT WORKS

The earth's gravity attracts objects downward. The heavier any object placed in the basket is, the more it weighs and the more it stretches the rubber band.

HEAVY OBJECT

LIGHT OBJECT

6 Test the weight of different objects by placing them in the basket. Heavy objects will cause the rubber band to stretch a lot and the basket to hang low down on the scale. Lighter weights will rest higher on the scale.

WEIGHING IN WATER

Take the rubber band and basket off the bottle top. Put an object in the basket and see how far it stretches the rubber band. Now lower the basket into a bucket of water. What happens to the basket and the rubber band? Is the rubber band still stretched by the same amount?

IN THE BALANCE

WHAT YOU NEED
Two beakers
String
Stiff cardboard
Ruler
Felt-tip pen
Coat hanger
Drinking straw
Tape

THE PREVIOUS PROJECT SHOWED you how to compare the weights of different objects one after the other. But the weight of an object can have another purpose. If you have an object that you know the weight of, you can use it to find the weight of other objects using an instrument called a balance. This project shows you how to make a simple balance.

BALANCING ACT

1 Ask an adult to pierce two holes in each beaker, one on either side near the top. Tie string to these holes to form long hoops.

2 Draw a scale on the cardboard using the pen and ruler. Make the central line longer so it stands out.

3 Tape the drinking straw to the underside of the coat hanger so that it points down.

4 Hang one beaker on each arm of the hanger and check that they are level when the hanger is hung up by its hook. Place the scale behind the hanger so the middle line sits behind the straw when the beakers are empty.

WHY IT WORKS

The hanger is a pivot around which the weights of the objects act. If the objects in the right-hand beaker weigh more, they exert more force on the coat hanger, causing the right side to hang lower.

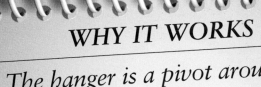

RIGHT-HAND BEAKER WEIGHS MORE

5 Compare the weights of different objects by placing them in each basket. See how much you need of different substances, such as water and sugar, before they balance.

COMPARING WEIGHTS

Get two objects which are the same size, but weigh different amounts, such as a tennis ball and a baseball. Place them in the beakers. The baseball will tip the balance because it is more dense.

FINDING THE MIDDLE

EVERY OBJECT HAS A CENTER OF GRAVITY. This is an imaginary point through which the weight of the object acts. In the last project, you saw how, by pivoting the coat hanger around its center of gravity, you were able to make it balance. At any other place, the pivot would not have been in line with the coat hanger's center of gravity, and would not have balanced. This project will show you how to find the center of gravity for any flat shape.

CENTER OF GRAVITY

1 *Ask an adult to cut out a random shape from the piece of cardboard.*

2 *Push one end of a length of string into a lump of modeling clay. Stick the thumbtack through the other end and push it through the cardboard shape. Pin the shape to the corkboard, making sure it can swing freely.*

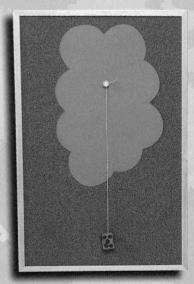

5 *Test your shape's center of gravity by balancing a sharp pencil upright, using modeling clay. Carefully place the shape on the pencil point where the lines cross. The shape will balance.*

WHY IT WORKS

When the string hangs from the same point as the cardboard, it passes through the cardboard's center of gravity. This is because weight always acts vertically down toward the center of the earth.

CENTER OF GRAVITY

3 Using the ruler, draw along the line made by the string as it hangs. Repeat a few times, pinning the shape in a different place each time.

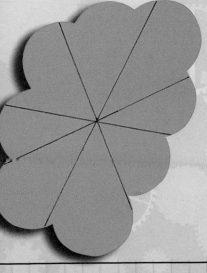

4 You will notice that the lines cross in one spot. This spot is the shape's center of gravity.

FANCY SHAPES

Cut out complex shapes from cardboard. Use the same method to find their center of gravity. Each time you pin the shapes, pin them as close to the edges as you can.

THE SANDS OF TIME

WHAT YOU
NEED
*Two small
bottles
Cardboard
Sharp pencil
Table salt
Watch or clock*

THERE IS ONE UNIT that is being used continuously and requires measuring all the time – and that's time! For thousands of years, people have measured the passing of time, using more and more complex methods to get more and more accurate readings. One of the earliest forms of time measurer, or clock, was the hourglass. This project shows you how to make your own simple hourglass.

HOURGLASS

2 *Pour some salt into the other bottle.*

1 *Make a tube from a strip of cardboard that will fit snugly over the necks of the bottles. Slide it over the top of one bottle. Ask an adult to cut out a small circle of cardboard to cover the mouth of the bottle and to make a small hole in the middle with a sharp pencil. Put the circle inside the tube so it covers the mouth of the bottle.*

3 *Turn the bottle with the tube upside-down and slide it over the mouth of the bottle containing the salt. Check the cardboard tube fits snugly.*

4 *Turn the bottles over, so the bottle with the salt is on top. The salt will start pouring into the bottom bottle.*

WHY IT WORKS

5 Using a watch or clock, time how long it takes for all the salt to flow from one bottle to the next. When this has happened, turn the bottles over and repeat. You will find that the time is exactly the same.

Gravity makes the salt fall into the bottom bottle. The flow of salt is slowed by the small hole which the salt has to pass through. As the amount of salt and the size of the hole remain the same, the time it takes the salt to flow from one bottle to the next will stay the same, however many times you repeat the project.

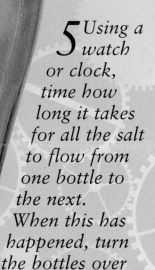

TIME RUNNING OUT

Make another form of timekeeper using a cardboard funnel, shown here. This time, mark lines on the side of the bottle. Read off where the top of the pile of salt is after each minute.

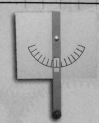

MEASURING SPEED

THE SPEED OF THINGS is referred to in several places in this book. Speed is the rate at which a distance is covered. This project shows how you can compare the different speeds of the air as it moves around you — what we call wind.

WIND SPEED

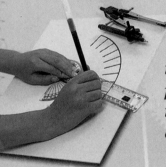

1 Draw a curved scale onto cardboard using the compass and the felt-tip pen. Mark equal points on the scale so you can compare wind speeds.

2 Ask an adult to cut out a strip of cardboard with a small window in it so you can see the scale.

WATCH THE WINDOW

Make another wind-speed measurer by tying strips of thick cardboard, thin cardboard, tinfoil, paper, and tissue paper to a stick, in that order. Start with the thick cardboard at the bottom. A weak wind will only move the tissue paper, but it will take a strong wind to move all the strips including the thick one.

3 Tape the Ping-Pong ball to one end of the cardboard strip. Pin the other end of the strip onto the sheet of cardboard on the spot where the point of the compass made a small hole. Make sure the strip can swing freely.

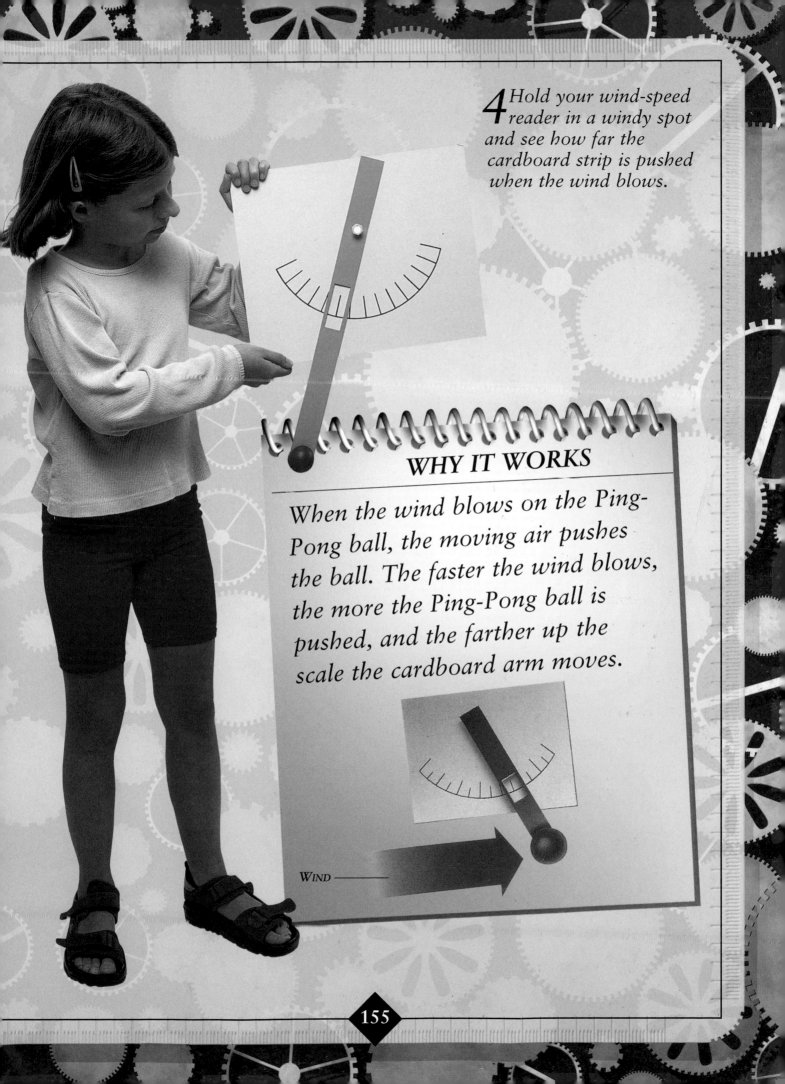

4 Hold your wind-speed reader in a windy spot and see how far the cardboard strip is pushed when the wind blows.

WHY IT WORKS

When the wind blows on the Ping-Pong ball, the moving air pushes the ball. The faster the wind blows, the more the Ping-Pong ball is pushed, and the farther up the scale the cardboard arm moves.

WIND

CHAPTER 8

WORK & SIMPLE MACHINES

INTRODUCTION

Simple machines are all around us all the time — even parts of our bodies work like simple machines. Machines are used to overcome forces, such as friction or gravity. However complicated they may seem, most machines are made up of just a few central parts, including levers, wheels, and pulleys. A seesaw is a type of lever. In this chapter the projects will show you how simple machines can make work easier to do.

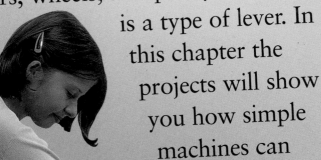

CONTENTS

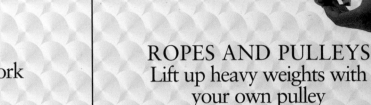

LEVERS

WHAT YOU NEED
*Colored
cardboard
Drinking straws
Marble
Cork, Tape
Scissors
Thumbtacks
Modeling clay*

MACHINES ARE DEVICES that make work easier. One of the most common machines is a lever. A lever is simply an arm that can move an object with the help of a pivot. We use levers all the time every day. A spade, a bottle opener, and even our arms and legs, are levers. This project shows you how to build a contraption that uses three different types of lever. Ask an adult to help you with all the steps.

FULL FORCE

1 *For the first lever, cut out a pointing hand and tape it to a length of straw, as shown here. Use modeling clay to attach this to one end of a strip of cardboard. Tape a short length of straw to the bottom of the strip (A).*

2 *For the second lever, make a tall box out of cardboard so that it is the same height as the pointing hand. Fold another strip of cardboard to make a channel for the marble to run along.*

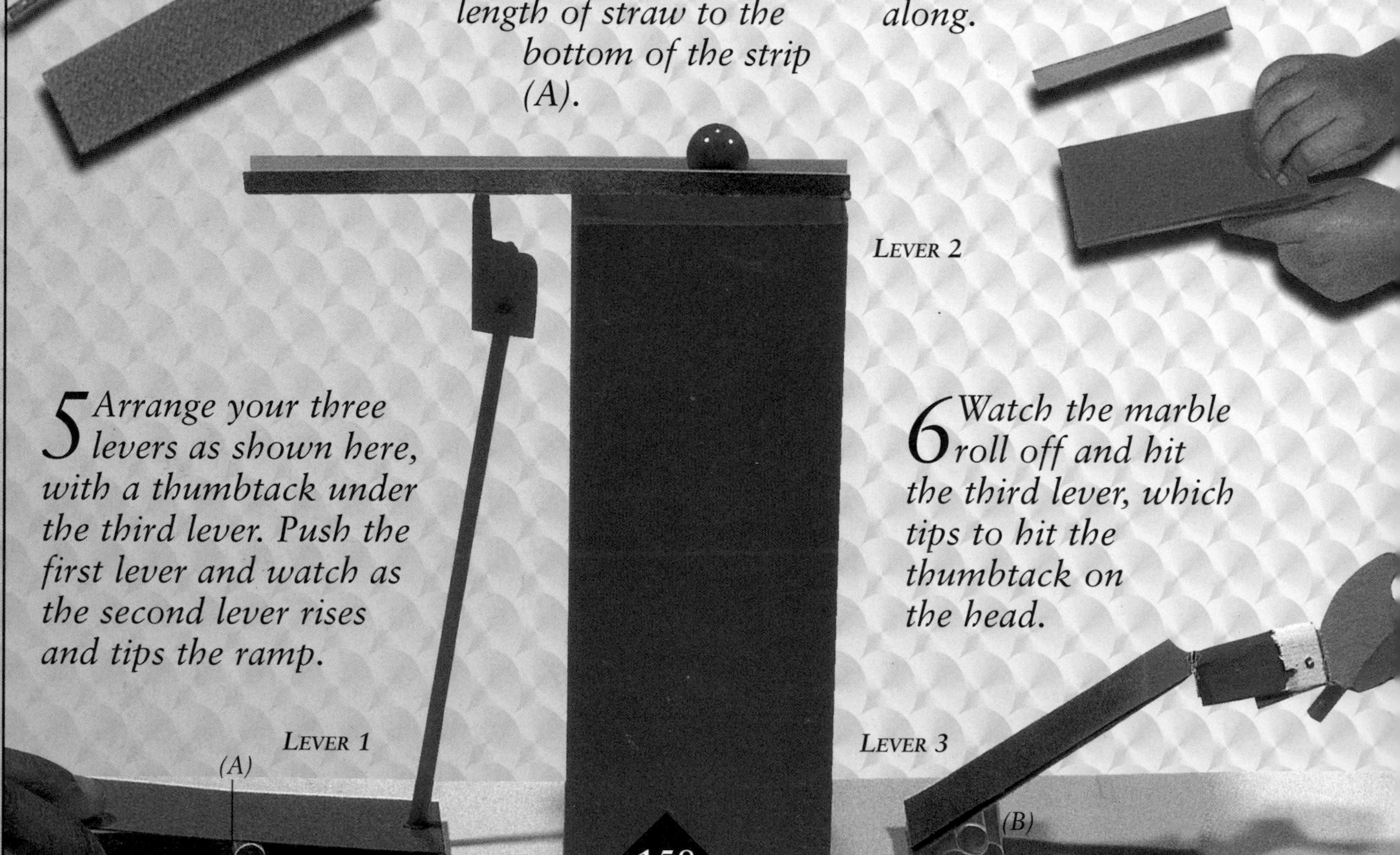

LEVER 2

5 *Arrange your three levers as shown here, with a thumbtack under the third lever. Push the first lever and watch as the second lever rises and tips the ramp.*

6 *Watch the marble roll off and hit the third lever, which tips to hit the thumbtack on the head.*

LEVER 1

(A)

LEVER 3

(B)

158

3 Tape one end of the cardboard channel to one side of the top of the tall box. Make sure the other end of the channel can move up and down easily.

4 For the third lever, make a hammer using a piece of straw, a thumbtack, and a cork, as shown. Cut out another pointing hand, tape it to the hammer, and attach it to another cardboard strip with clay. Now form a pyramid with three short lengths of straw and tape it to the bottom of the strip (B).

WHICH LEVER?

What types of lever are shown here? Look for other levers that are used at home. See if you can figure out what types of levers they are.

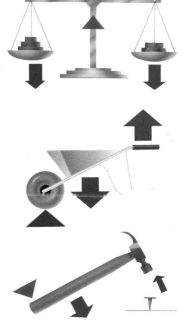

WHY IT WORKS

Your machine uses all three levers. The type of lever depends on where you find the pivot, the load, and the force needed to move it. A first-class lever (1) has the pivot between the force and the load. A second-class lever (2) has the load between the pivot and the force. A third-class lever (3) has the force between the load and the pivot.

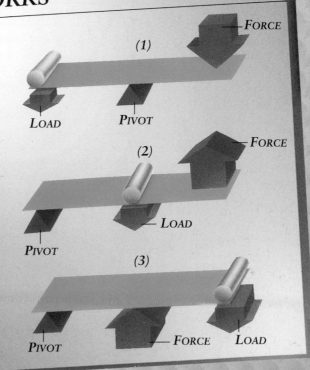

WORKING IN PAIRS

WHAT YOU NEED
Colored cardboard
Cardboard boxes
Paper fasteners
Thumbtacks
Glue
Used matchstick
Cotton thread
Rubber band
Drinking straw
Stapler
Scissors

SOMETIMES ONE LEVER is not enough to do a job. Scissors use two levers against each other to cut through an object, just as a pair of pliers uses two to grip something. You even find levers working in pairs on your own body. Pick up a pencil and you will see your fingers and thumb working against each other to grip the pencil. Build your own grabber in this project to see levers working in pairs.

LEVERS IN PAIRS

1 *Ask an adult to cut out three strips and a circle of cardboard with a slit in it, as shown. For the grabber's arm, glue two strips together as shown and attach the last strip with a paper fastener. For the base, glue together two boxes and decorate them with colored cardboard.*

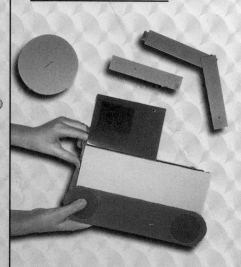

2 *Cut out two cardboard jaws. Attach the bottom set to the top set with a paper fastener. Glue the top set to the arm so the bottom set can still move. Glue a matchstick to the top set, as shown. Tie a long piece of thread to the matchstick.*

3 *Run the thread along the arm, through two lengths of straw, glued on as shown. Staple the rubber band to the arm and the bottom jaws to keep the jaws open.*

4 *Bend a length of straw and push it through the body. Tape the end of the thread to the straw to make a handle. Make sure it can turn.*

WHY IT WORKS

As you wind the handle, you reel in the thread, shortening it. This exerts a force on the arm. The parts of the arm act as levers, straightening around the pivot made by the paper fastener. The force is transmitted along the arm to the lower jaws, which also act as a lever.

LOOK FOR LEVERS

Look around your home to see other levers working in pairs. You will find them in scissors or tweezers. See if you can work out where the pivot is in each case.

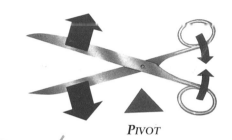

PIVOT

5 Tack the circle with the slit in it to the base, as shown. This is your turntable, so make sure it can move.

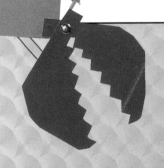

6 Slot the grabber's arm into the slit in the turntable. Turn the handle and watch as the arm straightens and the jaws close.

FRICTION

WHAT YOU NEED
Stiff cardboard
Wide and narrow drinking straws
Rubber band
Paper fasteners
Paints
Toothpick
Glue
Scissors

FOR MACHINES TO DO WORK, they must overcome certain forces. One of these forces is friction. Friction occurs when two things rub against each other. When you ride your bike, there is friction between the bike and the road and also between the bike, yourself, and the air. This has the effect of slowing you down. This project lets you see how friction slows some objects more than others.

WARMING UP

Rub your hands and they start to feel warm. As they rub against each other, the roughness of your hands creates friction. Energy lost in overcoming the friction shows itself as heat, and your hands feel warm.

WHY IT WORKS

Friction occurs between the objects and the strip, making the objects slow and stop. The amount of friction is affected by the weight, the smoothness, and the area of the object in contact with the strip. Heavy, rough, or large objects cause more friction and do not travel as far as light, smooth, or small objects.

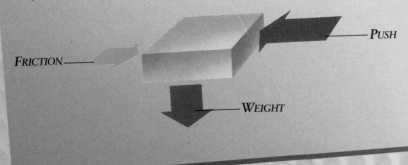

FRICTION ————

PUSH

WEIGHT

MOVING THINGS

1 Paint stripes across a long strip of cardboard. Cut and glue a short length of wide drinking straw in the middle of one end, as shown.

2 Make a T-shaped hammer by sticking two narrow straws together. Slide this into the wide straw stuck to the cardboard strip.

3 Push the toothpick sideways through the narrow straw. Push fasteners through the strip on either side of the hammer, as shown. Cut open a rubber band. Stretch it between the fasteners, hooking it behind the narrow straw.

4 Pull the hammer back and place an object in front of it. Release the hammer and see how far it manages to push the object along the strip.

5 Try several different objects and see how far your hammer pushes them along the strip of cardboard. Which objects travel the farthest and which travel the least?

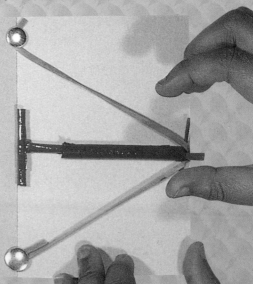

CLIMB THE HILL

WHAT YOU NEED
Stiff cardboard
Candle
Rubber bands
Toothpick
Thread spool
Tape
Drinking straw
Ruler
Scissors

THE LAST PROJECT SHOWED HOW friction is one of the forces involved when dealing with machines, and how it can slow objects down. However, friction does have its uses. Without friction you would not be able to stop when you ride your bike. You need the friction between the brake pads and your bike's wheels to slow you down. This project shows you another way that friction can be useful.

CLIMBING TANK

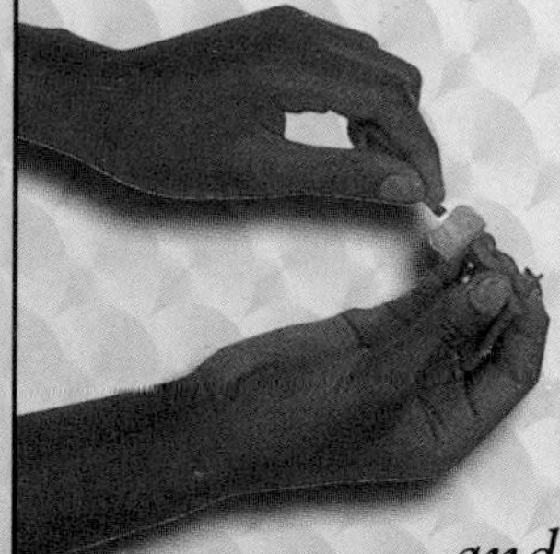

1 *Ask an adult to cut a short length off a candle and bore a hole through it. Push a rubber band through this hole and hold it in place with a toothpick, as shown.*

2 *Push the other end of the rubber band through the thread spool and secure it in place with tape.*

3 *Make a ramp from stiff cardboard (see page 172). Wind the toothpick as tight as it will go. Place the spool at the bottom of the ramp and see if it climbs up.*

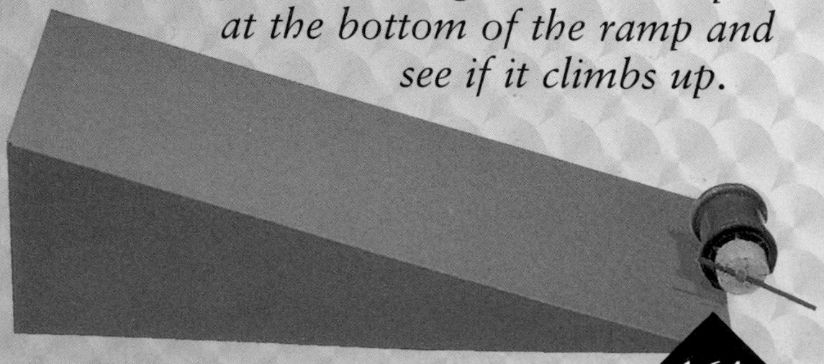

4 *Now attach some rubber band tires around the thread spool. Repeat the process and you will find that the spool can climb the ramp better this time.*

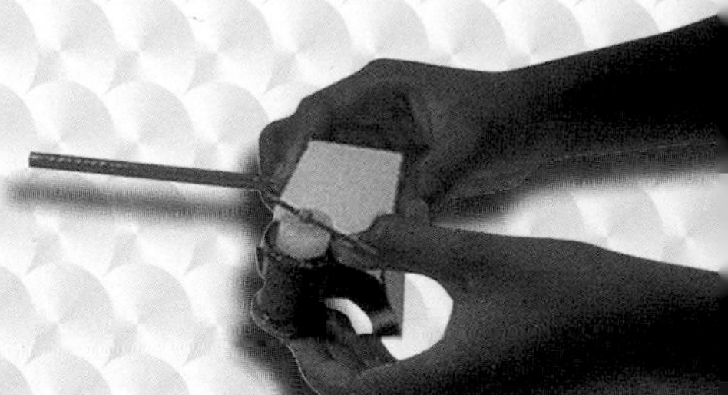

5 *Cut out a body shape for your tank from cardboard. Tape on a drinking straw for a gun. Fold the cardboard tank over the spool, as shown above.*

WHY IT WORKS

The tank uses the friction between the rubber bands and the slope to give it the grip to climb. Without these tires, there would not be enough friction to create enough grip for the tank to climb the slope. On the other hand, the candle wax reduces the friction between the toothpick and the thread spool, so the spool can spin more steadily as the rubber band unwinds. Without the candle wax, there might be too much friction for the spool to spin.

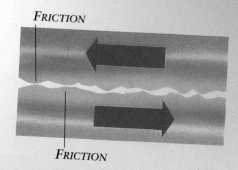

FRICTION

FRICTION

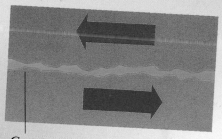

CANDLE WAX REDUCES FRICTION

6 Place your tank at the bottom of the ramp, wind the toothpick, and watch as your tank climbs the slope.

STEEPER SLOPE

How steep a slope can your tank climb? Try different sizes of rubber bands. Do thick or thin ones give the best grip?

WHEEL AND AXLE

WHAT YOU NEED
Colored cardboard
Stiff cardboard
Four round sponges
Scissors
Wooden sticks
Tape
Glue
Strong drinking straws

WHEELS ARE GOOD FOR MOVING OBJECTS because their round shape reduces the area of contact between surfaces and so reduces friction. However, a vehicle needs more than rigid wheels if it is to be useful. To get around corners, these wheels need to turn. Early carts used a simple axle to achieve this. See how one works in this project.

STEER CLEAR

1 *Ask an adult to cut out a steering wheel and two car shapes from colored cardboard, as shown, for the sides of the car. Leave spaces for the wheels, but make sure you leave flaps hanging from the back wheel arches, as shown. Glue more cardboard on for the windows.*

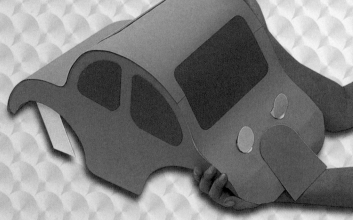

GOING BACKWARD

Try pushing your car in reverse and steering. You will notice that the car follows a different path when the wheels are steering from the back.

2 *Ask an adult to cut a wide strip of cardboard for the car body. Tape the body to the sides, under the car. Turn it upside down to do this. Glue on windows, headlights, and a radiator flap at the front.*

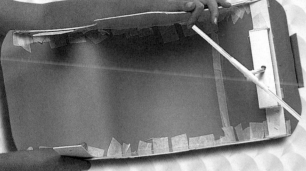

3 Make a steering column and axle by sticking two straws together with lots of tape, as shown.

4 Turn the car over. At the front end, stick a strip of stiff cardboard between the sides of the car, with another strip on top, as shown. Ask an adult to push the T-shaped straws through both strips and through the body of the car.

5 Make the wheels by sticking a circle of cardboard on each sponge. For the front wheels, push a stick into one sponge. Thread the stick through the T-shaped part of the axle you made with straws. Then stick another wheel on the other end.

WHY IT WORKS

By turning the steering wheel, you are moving the axle and the wheels away from the straight-on path of the car. Because the car then has to follow the new path that the wheels are pointing in, the car turns a corner.

6 For the back wheels, thread a stick through the hanging flaps and stick a sponge on each end. Tape on your steering wheel, and off you go!

LIFTING A LOAD

THE PREVIOUS PROJECT SHOWED you how wheels can be useful in machines to reduce friction. However, wheels can also be used for other important tasks. A machine called a winch is basically a wheel which, when turned, winds up a length of rope to lift something. You can see this in action with a mini water well which you can make in this project.

WHAT YOU NEED
*Stiff and colored
cardboard
Drinking straws
Wooden stick
String
Glue
Tape
Scissors*

WHY IT WORKS

The shape of the handle means that your hand moves a greater distance than the distance turned by the straw. This reduces the amount of work you do, but means you do the work over a longer distance.

Learn about this using slopes and pulleys in the next projects.

WINDING POWERS

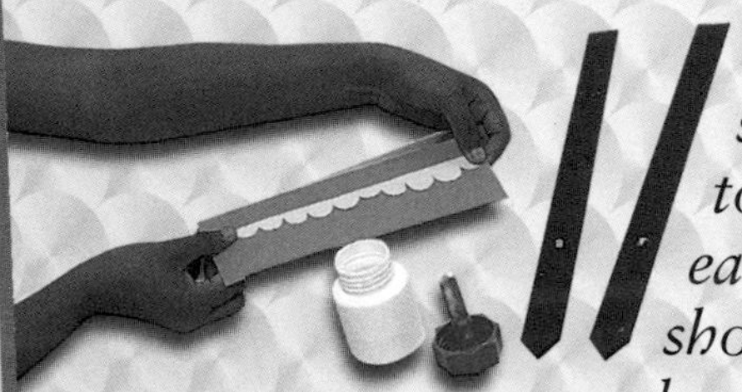

1 Ask an adult to cut two strips of stiff cardboard and to punch a hole in each of them, as shown. Cut out and decorate a roof shape from colored cardboard.

2 Ask an adult to cut out a cardboard ring, as shown here, and to cut a slit on each side just wide enough to hold the cardboard strips.

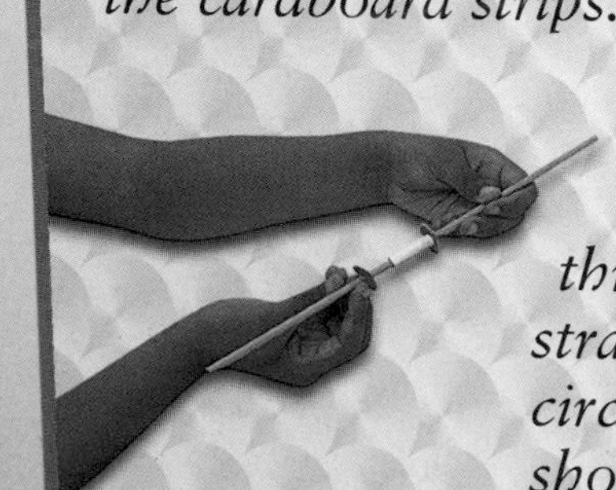

3 Ask an adult to thread a stick through a small piece of straw and two small circles of cardboard, as shown. Hold it in place with tape.

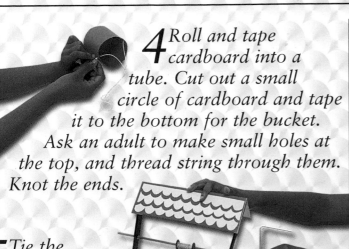

4 Roll and tape cardboard into a tube. Cut out a small circle of cardboard and tape it to the bottom for the bucket. Ask an adult to make small holes at the top, and thread string through them. Knot the ends.

5 Tie the bucket onto the small piece of straw, so that it will wind up, as shown. Push the stick through the holes in the cardboard strips. Bend a straw into a handle shape and thread it onto the end of the stick. Make sure it can turn easily. Tape on the roof shape you made earlier.

MAKING IT EASIER

Make the length of the handle longer. You will find it even easier to wind up the bucket. This is because your hand moves even farther than before, so the amount of work is less.

6 Make a well base in the same way you made the bucket, so that the ring fits on top. Slot the cardboard strips through the slits in the ring and tape them to the inside of the base. Turn the handle and watch the bucket wind up.

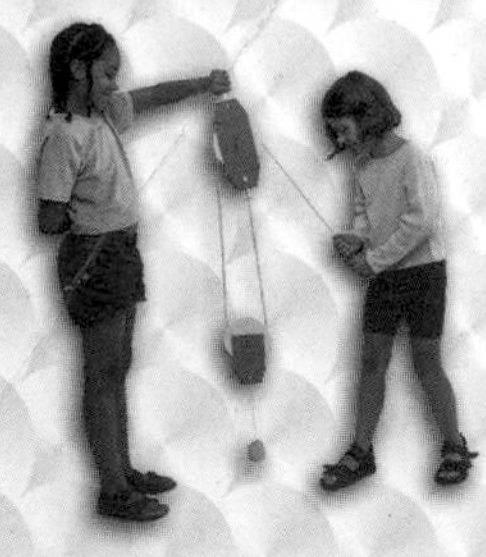

*R*OPES AND PULLEYS

WHAT YOU NEED
Colored cardboard
Glue, String
Drinking straws
Scissors
Modeling clay

THE LAST PROJECT SHOWED how winches and handles can reduce the level of work you do by increasing the distance over which it is done. Other machines used to reduce the level of work are pulleys. These are systems of wheels which, when ropes are wrapped around them, increase the distance greatly and so reduce the work level. You can build your own pulley system in this project.

HANGING AROUND

For another pulley, thread some string between two coat hangers. The more you thread the string between the hangers, the easier it is to lift a load. But you have to pull for longer each time, so the total work done is the same.

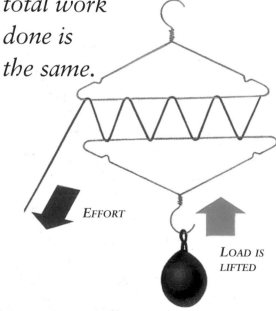

EFFORT
LOAD IS LIFTED

PULLING IT UP

1 Ask an adult to cut out the cardboard shapes shown here and to punch holes through the middle of the circles and on the other pieces of cardboard, as shown.

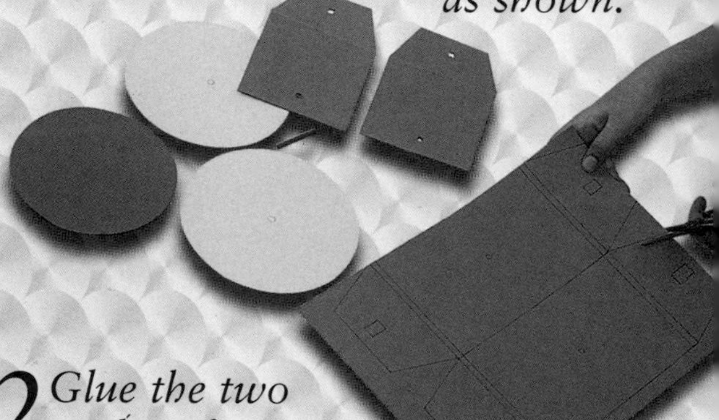

2 Glue the two circles of cardboard together, with a smaller circle of thick cardboard between them to make a thick wheel. Make another of these wheels.

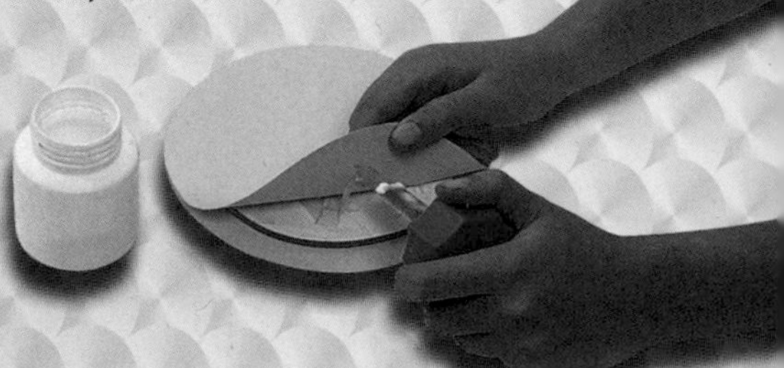

By using two pulleys, you double the distance you have to pull with one pulley. This halves the work level and makes lifting the load easier. But you have to work for twice as long, so the total work done is the same.

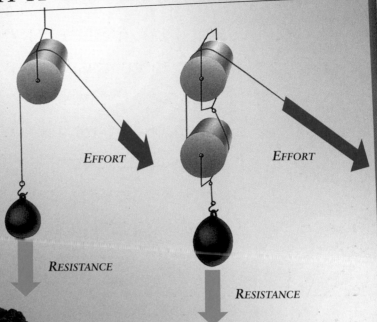

EFFORT

EFFORT

RESISTANCE

RESISTANCE

3 Sandwich each wheel between the cardboard shapes you cut out, as shown, and push a drinking straw through the holes in each to make your pulleys. Attach a handle to one pulley and a lump of modeling clay to the other.

4 Tie the string to the bottom of the pulley with the handle, thread it around the wheel of the other pulley, and then up over the wheel of the first pulley, as shown. Pull on this end of the pulley and watch as the load rises.

Up the Hill

WHAT YOU NEED
*Stiff, colored
cardboard
Toy car
String
Drinking straws
Tape, Glue
Modeling clay
Ruler
Scissors*

YOU MIGHT FIND walking up a slope hard work, but have you ever wondered how hard it would be to climb the same height as the slope, only vertically (straight up)? You may travel less distance, but the effort required is a lot greater. You can compare how much easier a slope makes it to climb a height in this project.

PULLING POWER

1 *Ask an adult to help you make a ramp by cutting and folding a piece of cardboard as shown. Use the ruler and scissors to score a sharp fold line.*

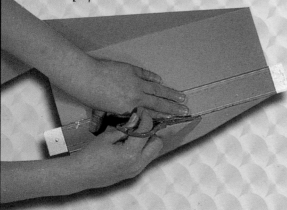

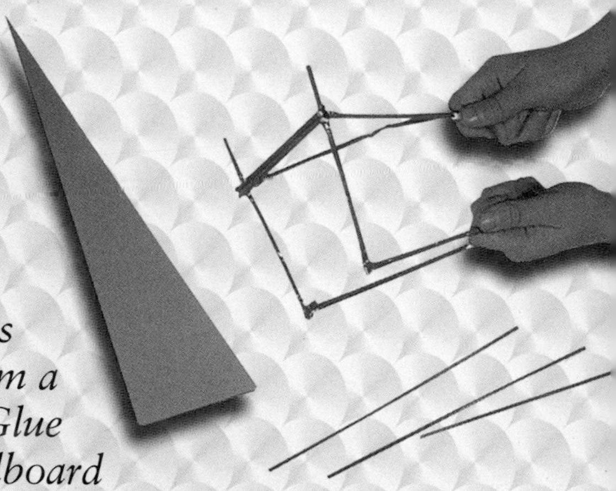

2 *Tape the straws together to form a frame as shown. Glue on squares of cardboard to strengthen the frame, as shown opposite. Push a lump of modeling clay onto a piece of string, and cover it with cardboard to make a bucket. Tie the other end of the string to the toy car.*

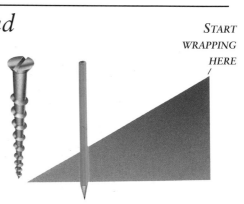

SCREWING IT UP

Screws are basically slopes that are wound around a central point. Test this by taking a triangular piece of paper and wrapping it around a pencil. Start at the shortest side of the triangle. The paper forms a screw pattern around the pencil.

START
WRAPPING
HERE

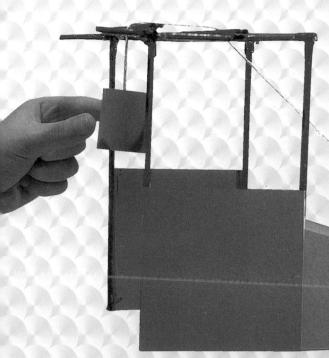

3 Place the drinking straw frame at the top of the slope. Put the car at the bottom of the slope and run the string over the frame. Add more modeling clay to your bucket until there is enough weight to pull the car up the slope.

4 Now place the car directly under the frame. Add more modeling clay to your bucket. You will find that much more weight is needed to raise the car vertically.

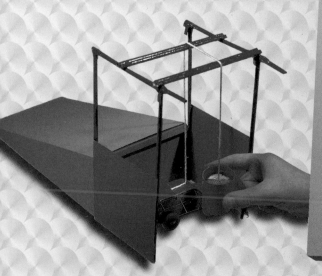

WHY IT WORKS

By moving the angle of work away from the vertical, a slope reduces the effects of gravity and reduces the level of work done. At the same time, however, it increases the distance the load has to move.
So the total work done is the same.

WHEELS AND COGS

WHAT YOU NEED
Colored cardboard
Corrugated
cardboard, Glue
Ping-Pong balls
Cardboard box
Wooden sticks
Straws, Scissors

IN OTHER PROJECTS, you have seen how machines can be used to transmit power. One way of transmitting power is by using gears. The most common gear is the cog — a wheel with teeth. You may have seen cogs on a bicycle. Build some cogs and see the effects of using different sizes.

MAKING COGS

1 *Ask an adult to cut out pairs of cardboard circles and thin strips from the corrugated cardboard. Glue the pairs of circles together with a strip of corrugated cardboard between them. Make sure that the ribbed side of the corrugated cardboard is facing out. These are your cogs.*

2 *Push a piece of stick through a hole in the center of each cog, so that it comes out the other side. Push a Ping-Pong ball stuck on a straw through a hole in the edge of each cog, as shown.*

WHY IT WORKS

Because the ribs of each cog interlock, when you turn the first cog, the turning force is transmitted to the second cog, causing it to turn. If you turn the smaller cog one rotation, the larger wheel will not rotate as much. But if you turn the larger cog once, the smaller cog turns more than once.

3 Make holes in a cardboard box and push the wooden sticks through them. Ask an adult to help you.

4 Make sure the two cogs are touching each other and that the corrugated ribs interlock.

5 Decorate the box with colored cardboard.

ADDING COGS

Add a third cog to your system of gears and look at what happens. You will find that the final wheel turns in the same direction as the first wheel.

6 Turn one cog. The other cog turns as well, but in the opposite direction. Count how many times the second cog turns for every turn of the first cog. Try cogs of different sizes and see how this affects the number of turns of each one.

CHAPTER 9

SHAPES & STRUCTURES

INTRODUCTION

From a piece of cloth to the most complex bridge, every object, large or small, has a shape and a structure. Some shapes fit together better than others, and some materials are stronger than others. Read on and discover the properties of different materials. Find out which shapes and which materials are best for building strong structures, such as skyscrapers and bridges.

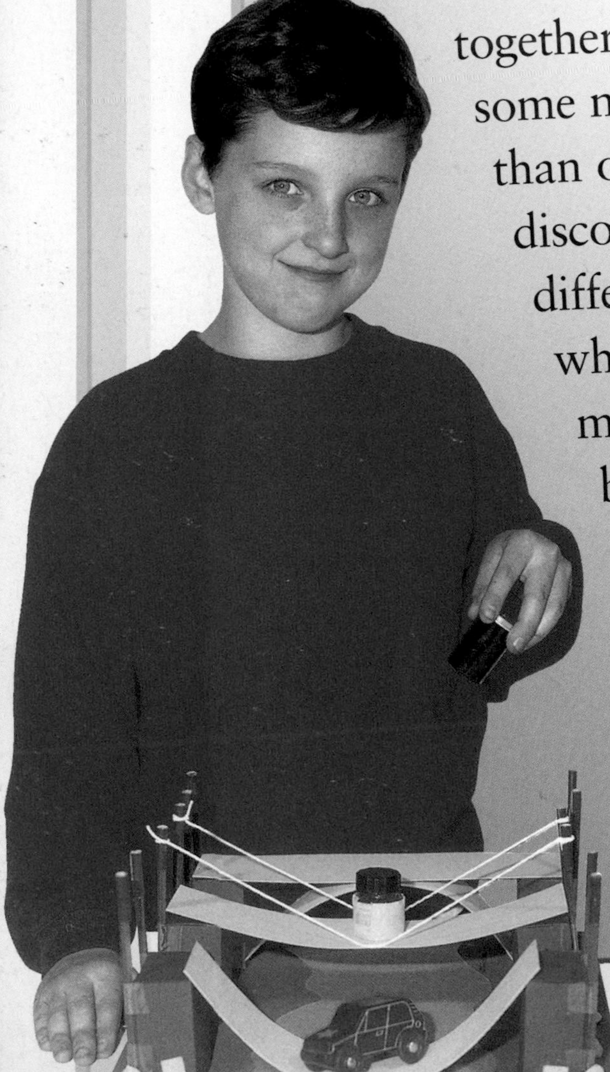

CONTENTS

HANDLING HEAT

WHAT YOU NEED
Toothpicks
Paper
Tape
Colored pencils
Metal lid
Plastic lid
Wooden disk
Cooking fat
Large bowl
Hot water
Watch

IN DECIDING WHICH MATERIALS to use when making something, designers and engineers must decide which materials are best suited to a particular job. For example, it would be no good making a saucepan out of plastic, because it would melt as soon as you put it on the stove. Sometimes they may even need to test various materials to find out which works best for the task. This project lets you test several materials to find out which is the best at conducting heat.

FEEL THE HEAT

1 Cut out three pieces of paper the same size. Tape each piece of paper to a toothpick to make three flags. Decorate each flag differently using colored pencils.

KEEPING IT HOT

Collect cups made of different materials, such as metal, plastic, and china. Fill each of these with the same amount of hot water. Leave for several minutes. Then, using a thermometer, find out which cup is the best at keeping the water hot.

2 Cut three lumps of cooking fat that are the same size. Place one lump on each of the metal and plastic lids and the wooden disk. Push a flag into each lump of fat.

WHY IT WORKS

The flag on the metal lid drops first because the tiny molecules which make up the lid conduct heat very well (1). Heat energy from the water passes quickly from one molecule to the next, until it reaches the fat, causing it to melt. The flag on the wooden disk (2) will be the last to drop because wood molecules are bad heat conductors.

(2)

(1)

3 Ask an adult to fill a large bowl with hot water. Place the lids and the disk in the bowl so that they float.

4 Using a watch, time how long it takes for each lump of fat to melt and each flag to drop. Which of the three flags drops first and which drops last?

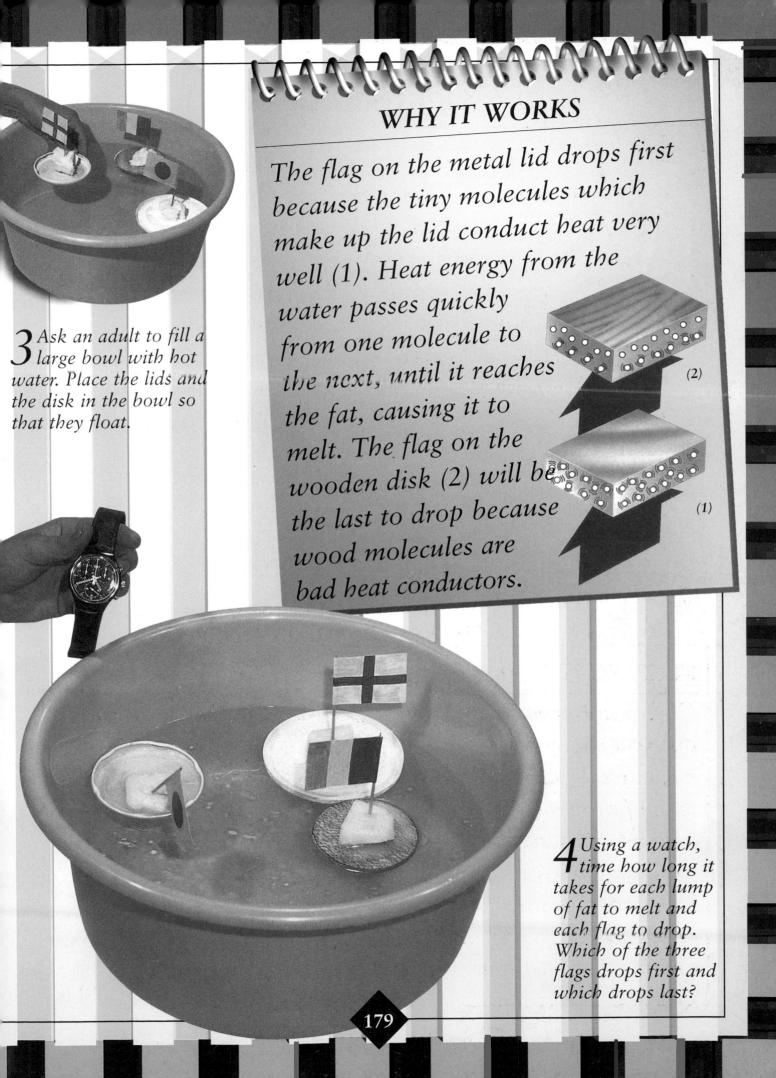

TESTING MATERIALS

WHAT YOU NEED
Paper
Tissue paper
Plastic bag
Scissors, Tape
Wooden dowels
Three plastic cups
String
Marbles
Colored cardboard

THE LAST PROJECT SHOWED how to test materials to see which was the best conductor of heat. Another important property of a material is its strength. A material must be strong enough for the job it has to do — one that breaks under the slightest pressure may be dangerous if used for the wrong thing. This project shows how to find which of three materials can carry the heaviest load.

WHY IT WORKS

The plastic bag strip can carry the most weight because the tiny molecules that make up the plastic are held together by very strong bonds. The tissue paper is the weakest strip because it is made up of fibers that are not very densely packed and come apart easily.

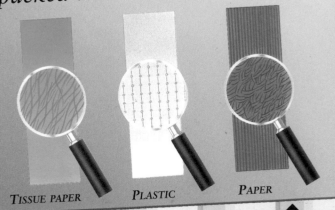

TISSUE PAPER   PLASTIC   PAPER

CARRYING THE LOAD

1 Cut three strips from the paper, the tissue paper, and the plastic bag. Make sure that they are all the same width.

2 Tape one wooden dowel to the top and bottom of each strip.

3 Cut some string and tie it in a big loop. Cross the middle of the loop over the bottom of each of the plastic cups and tape it in place, as shown.

4 Loop a cup over one of the dowels on each strip, as shown. Tie another string loop to the dowel at the other end of each strip.

STRIP TESTING

Repeat the test with three strips of different widths of the same plastic. Which carries the most weight?

5 Make a stand from colored cardboard and push three dowels through it, as shown. Hang the strips from the dowels. Add marbles to the cups until the strips break. Which one breaks first?

SPRINGY MATERIALS

WHAT YOU NEED
Stiff wire
Ping-Pong ball
Tape
Paper and cloth
Pipe cleaners
Paint
Bottle cap
Cardboard box
Empty spray can
Thick cardboard tube
Scissors

YOU MIGHT HAVE NOTICED that some materials, no matter how much you stretch, crush, bend, or twist them, will always go back to their original shape and size. Sometimes it is important to use flexible materials like this. For example, a plane's wings are designed to bend a little to absorb the force exerted on them by flying. This project lets you have fun with a material's flexibility.

JACK-IN-THE-BOX

1 Make a spring by coiling stiff wire around the empty spray can.

2 Paint a face on the Ping-Pong ball. Tape a pipe cleaner to the bottom of the ball for your jack's body. Make a hat from some cloth.

3 Tape the bottom of the pipe cleaner body to a bottle cap. Tightly wind one end of the spring around the bottle cap. Use pipe cleaners to make arms. Make clothes and gloves from cloth.

4 Decorate the cardboard box using the paints.

5 Tape a short piece of the thick cardboard tube to the bottom of the box. Make sure the spring fits snugly inside the tube.

WHY IT WORKS

Most materials have elasticity — they can resume their shape after being squashed. In a spring at rest (1), all the forces acting on it are balanced. Squeezing increases the forces that make the spring want to spring apart (2). Releasing the spring causes it to push apart again.

(1)

(2)

HANGING DOWN

Fix a weight to end of a ruler. Hang it over the edge of a table. Now move the ruler so it hangs further over the edge. Does it bend more?

6 Put the spring inside the tube, then push the jack down into the box, and close the lid. Open the lid quickly and watch the jack spring up out of the box.

WEAVING MATERIALS

SOME MATERIALS ARE ONLY strong in one direction and so are not good to use in structures by themselves. One way around this weakness is to weave strands of material together. This creates a new structure that has strengths in all directions. Clothing fibers are an example of this. They combine threads to create usable materials. Learn how to weave strands of yarn in this project.

WHAT YOU NEED
Cardboard
Scissors
String
Colored yarn
Wooden dowels

WHY IT WORKS

The strings running up and down your loom are called warp threads. The yarn strands that you weave across the loom are called weft threads. By weaving the threads together, the finished fabric is strong. The closer the weave, the stronger the fabric.

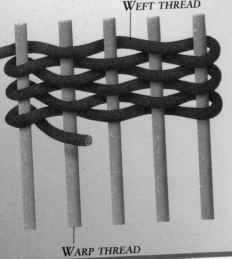

WEFT THREAD

WARP THREAD

SMOOTH FIBERS

Have a look at the ends of different threads of material with a magnifying glass. Compare the sizes of each fiber and see how smooth the ends are.

MAKE A LOOM

1 To make your loom, ask an adult to cut an odd number of notches along the top and bottom of a piece of cardboard.

2 Wind a length of string around each pair of notches and knot each loop at the back of your loom.

3 Weave a strand of yarn in and out of each length of string. Make sure you push each row up into the one above it. To change color, tie your new yarn onto the end of the old strand.

4 When you have finished, knot the last piece of yarn and lift the fabric off your loom. Push two wooden dowels through the top and bottom of your material and hang it up as a decoration.

GETTING STRONGER

SOMETIMES, ONE MATERIAL ON ITS OWN is not suitable for a job, and two or more different materials may need to be combined to create the right material. Fiberglass, for example, contains tiny pieces of glass in a plastic, which makes it both flexible and strong. In this project, see how you can strengthen plaster of Paris by adding another material.

WHY IT WORKS

The block of plaster alone (1) is brittle and will break when a strong force is applied to it. The block that contains the metal wire (2) will last longer because it can bend a little and absorb the knocks it receives.

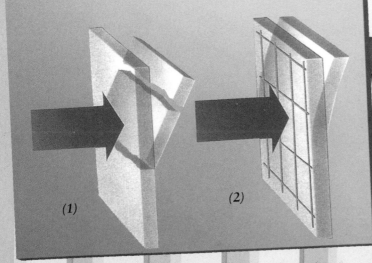

(1) (2)

REINFORCED PLASTER

1 Ask an adult to make a frame out of thick cardboard as shown. Mix the plaster of Paris with some water and pour into the frame.

2 When the block is dry, remove it from the frame. You need to make another block the same size, but before you start, lay some pieces of wire into the frame.

186

CLAY BRICKS

Make bricks out of clay and leave them to harden. Now make more bricks of the same size, but this time mix some straw into the clay. Test them for strength and find out which ones last the longest.

5 Swing the weight at the blocks of plaster. Make sure that you hit each block at the same spot and that you release the weight from the same distance each time.

3 Lay the wires both across and lengthwise, as shown here. Now make your second block of plaster with the wires embedded in it.

6 You will find that the block with the metal wire will last a lot longer before it shatters than the block without any wire.

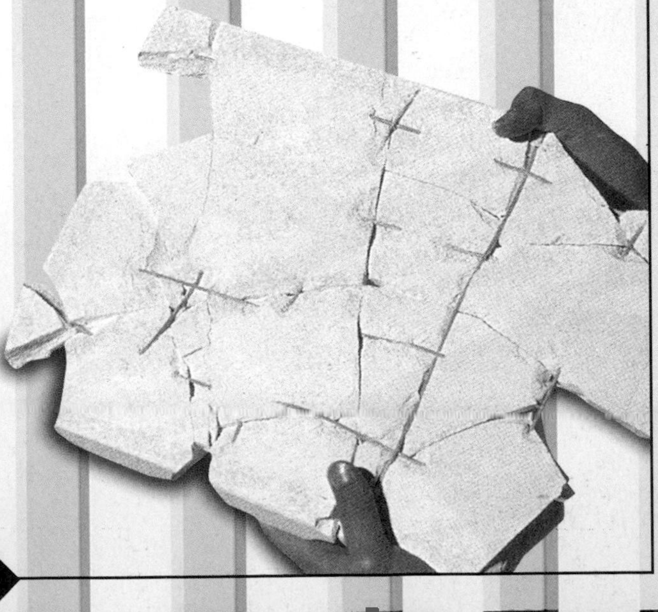

4 Ask an adult to cut out cardboard supports. Lean the blocks against these on a sheet of plastic, as shown. Tie a weight to a length of string. Tie up the string so that it can swing.

NATURAL STRUCTURES

WHAT YOU NEED
Plastic tray
Large bowl
Water
Modeling clay
Sand and soil
Green powder
paint
Model trees
Saw

SOME OF THE LARGEST and most impressive structures found on this planet are not made by humans at all. Instead, they have been formed naturally by the forces of the wind, sea, rivers, or even the movement of the massive plates of rock that make up the earth's surface. These structures include soaring mountains, enormous canyons, and towering waterfalls. This project shows you how a river can carve shapes and structures into the landscape.

FREEZING WATER

Water changes the shape of the land when it freezes. To see how, fill a plastic bottle with water. Screw the top on tightly. Put it in a sealed plastic bag in the freezer all night. The water expands as it freezes and shatters the plastic bottle.

7 *Slowly pour in water at the back of the tray. Watch it flow down the slope, carving a path into the sand and soil. Make sure you catch the water in a bowl.*

FLOWING RIVER

1 Ask an adult to saw off the front of a plastic tray.

2 Put some mounds of modeling clay around the bottom of the tray.

3 Pour the soil over the mounds so that they are covered. Make sure that the soil forms a slope from the back of the tray down to the open front.

4 Cover the soil with a layer of dry sand.

5 Now cover the sand with a layer of green powder paint to give a grass effect.

6 Add some model trees. Make a record of what it looks like by drawing or taking a photograph.

WHY IT WORKS

Water always flows down a slope (1). As it does so, it picks up soil particles and carries them along. The more soil it carries, the more it changes the landscape around it. Some rivers form huge bends called meanders (2). Over time, these bends are worn away, leaving small, crescent-shaped lakes called oxbow lakes (3).

189

TESTING SHAPES

YOU TESTED DIFFERENT TYPES of material for strength on pages 180–181. Strength is also an important factor when deciding if the shape of a structure suits a task. Tessellating shapes (shapes that fit together exactly) are strong and are good for covering an area. This project shows you how some shapes can be strong in one direction but very weak in another.

WHY IT WORKS

The shape of the tube means that it can take a lot of compressional (squeezing) force along its length. However, its sides are weak, and they will collapse when the slightest compressional force is placed on its side.

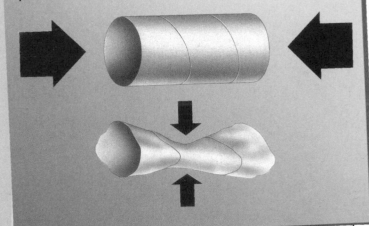

EGG STRENGTH

Repeat the project, but this time use an egg instead of the cardboard tube. You will find that, like the tube, the egg can bear more weight when it is standing upright (you will need some modeling clay to hold it in place) than when it is on its side.

1 Place a cardboard tube on its side. Stack coins on either side of the tube, until they are just below the width of the tube itself.

2 Place one of the books on top of the tube. Keep adding books until the tube collapses and the books rest on the stacks of coins.

3 Place the second tube on its end. Put plastic cups that are just smaller than the tube on either side.

4 Again place the books on top of the tube. See how many books have to be added before the tube collapses.

5 This time, you will find that you need more books before the tube collapses.

TALL STRUCTURES

WHEN PUTTING TOGETHER A BUILDING, engineers and designers have to be aware of the stresses and forces that the building might be subjected to over its lifetime. They must then find the best materials and shapes to keep the building upright. This project shows you one solution for coping with the large forces a tall skyscraper has to put up with.

WHAT YOU NEED
Ruler, Pen
Thick cardboard
Colored cardboard
Scissors
Glue

REACH FOR THE SKY

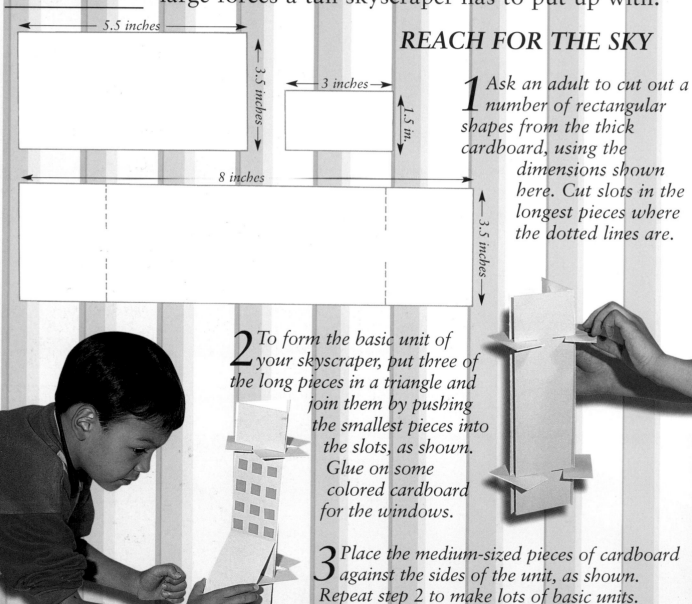

5.5 inches

3.5 inches

3 inches

1.5 in.

8 inches

3.5 inches

1 *Ask an adult to cut out a number of rectangular shapes from the thick cardboard, using the dimensions shown here. Cut slots in the longest pieces where the dotted lines are.*

2 *To form the basic unit of your skyscraper, put three of the long pieces in a triangle and join them by pushing the smallest pieces into the slots, as shown. Glue on some colored cardboard for the windows.*

3 *Place the medium-sized pieces of cardboard against the sides of the unit, as shown. Repeat step 2 to make lots of basic units.*

The medium-sized and square pieces of cardboard support the building by forming a broad base for each unit. This makes each level, and the structure as a whole, more stable. These triangular supporting structures are called buttresses.

CARD TOWER

Make a tower from playing cards. The triangular shape of each level is what makes the cards stable.

4 Cut out some squares of cardboard, measuring 3.5 in. along the sides. To build your skyscraper, stack the basic units on top of each other. At each level, lean the cardboard squares against the units, as shown.

5 See how high you can build your skyscraper.

BUILDING BRIDGES

WHAT YOU NEED
Wooden blocks
Pencils
Tape
Thick cardboard
String, Glue
Colored
cardboard
Modeling clay

THE LAST PROJECT SHOWED you how to build upward. But what happens if you have to build a structure that runs across something? Bridges give designers and engineers different problems. This project shows some of the ways that these problems can be overcome.

BRIDGING THE GAP

1 Tape pencils to two corners of each wooden block, as shown here.

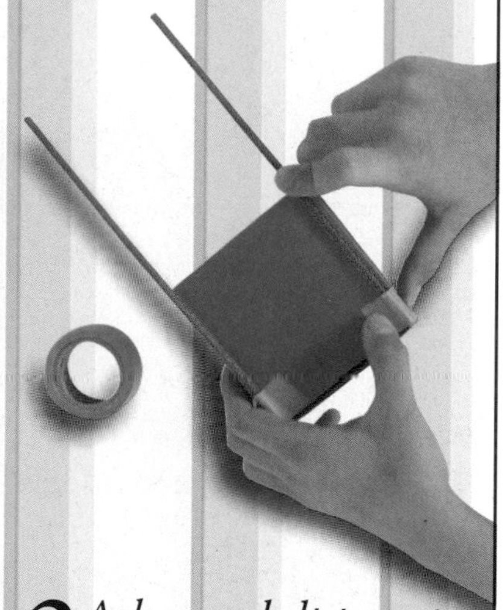

2 Ask an adult to cut out strips of thick cardboard the same width as the wooden blocks. For the first bridge, simply place one strip between two of the blocks.

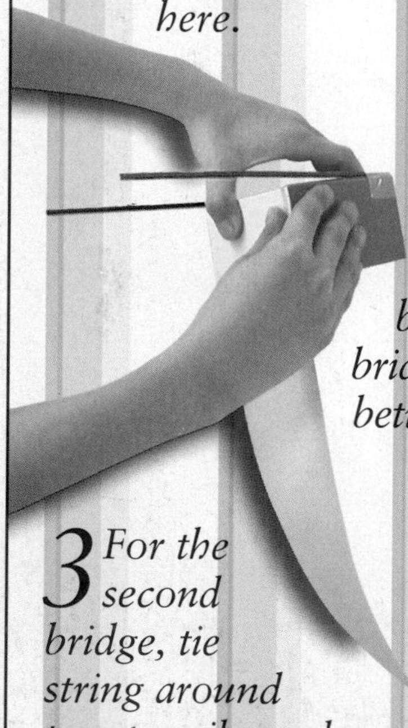

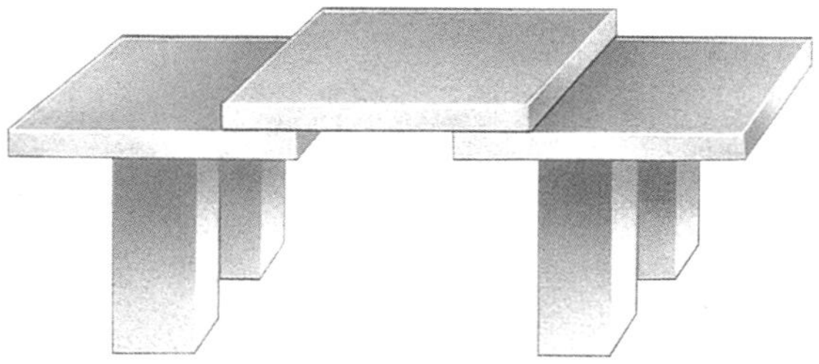

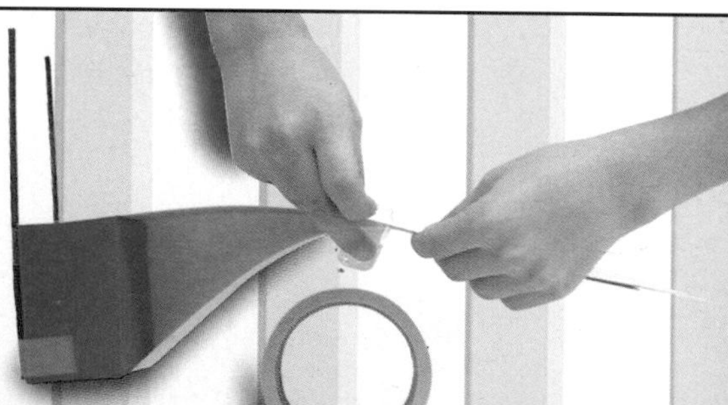

3 For the second bridge, tie string around two pencils, and tape it to the middle of a cardboard strip, as shown. Then tie it to the pencils on another block.

CANTILEVER BRIDGE

Another bridge structure is the cantilever bridge. Make your own cantilever bridge as shown here and see how much weight it can support.

4 For your third bridge, place another strip of cardboard under the first strip. Glue this to the wooden blocks and your bridge's roadway to form an arch.

194

WHY IT WORKS

Your first bridge will buckle quickly as it has no supporting structure for the road. The road held by the string, called a suspension bridge, will buckle next. The strongest bridge is the arch bridge. The arch shape is best at spreading any weight on the bridge over its whole length.

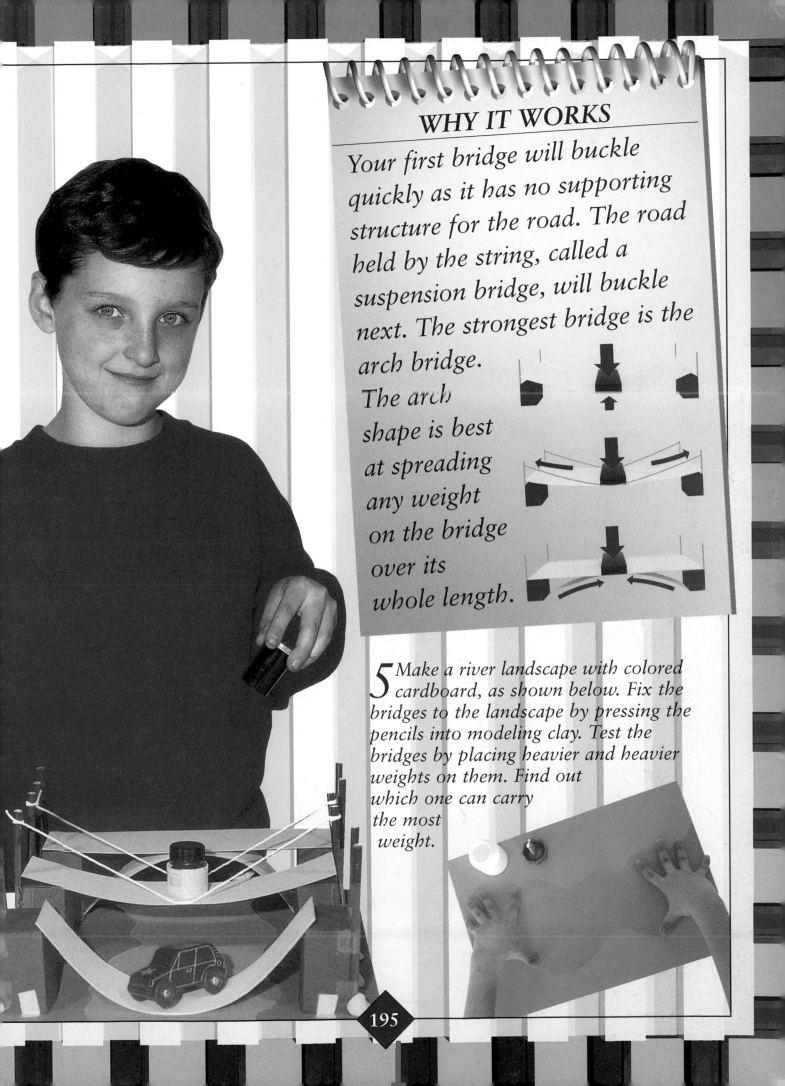

5 Make a river landscape with colored cardboard, as shown below. Fix the bridges to the landscape by pressing the pencils into modeling clay. Test the bridges by placing heavier and heavier weights on them. Find out which one can carry the most weight.

CHAPTER 10

CHEMICALS & REACTIONS

INTRODUCTION

Chemical reactions are happening around us and inside us all the time. When ice melts or water boils, a chemical reaction is taking place as the water changes from solid to liquid, or liquid to gas. This chapter looks at the basic aspects of everyday chemistry. By following the projects, you will learn about acids and alkalis, build an erupting volcano, and bake your own bread.

CONTENTS

WHAT YOU NEED
Two plastic drink bottles
Permanent felt-tip pen
Water
Measuring cup

FREEZING

WHEN THE WEATHER GETS REALLY COLD, you may have noticed that the water in puddles, ponds, and even streams turns solid. This solid water is called ice. As the temperature drops, a chemical reaction takes place that changes the structure of the water. We say that the water freezes, or solidifies, to form ice. Look at some of the differences between liquid water and solid ice in this project.

WHY IT WORKS

Water is made up of tiny molecules that float around at random when the water is liquid. When the water freezes, the molecules join into a box-like framework. This keeps the molecules at a greater distance from each other. As a result, water expands when it freezes and occupies a greater volume.

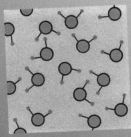

WATER

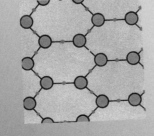

ICE

ICED WATER

Put an ice cube in a glass of water. Ice is made up of molecules that are more spaced-out than the molecules in the liquid water. The solid ice is less dense than the liquid water, and weighs less than the same volume of water. As a result, the ice floats on top of the water.

198

FEELING THE CHILL

1 Use a measuring cup to pour exactly the same amount of water into each of the plastic bottles.

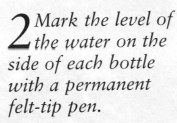

2 Mark the level of the water on the side of each bottle with a permanent felt-tip pen.

3 Place one bottle in the freezer and leave the other at room temperature in a place that is not too warm. Leave the two bottles overnight.

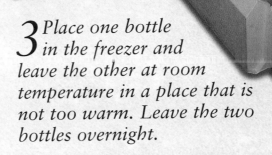

4 Take the bottle from the freezer and compare the levels of both bottles. You will see that the level in the bottle containing the ice is higher than in the bottle containing the liquid water.

DISSOLVING

WHAT YOU NEED
*Three drinking
glasses
Water
Measuring cup
Salt
Soil
Fine sand
Plastic cup*

IN THE LAST PROJECT, you looked at some of the differences between liquid and solid water. Liquid and solid are known as different states of water. One difference between the two states is that liquid water can absorb and hold certain substances within its structure, but solid ice cannot. This is a chemical reaction called dissolving. However, water cannot absorb every substance, as this project will show.

ONE SUGAR OR TWO?

Look around your home and see if you can find examples where water dissolves other substances. Ask an adult to pour hot water on sugar or instant coffee granules and see what happens.

NOW YOU SEE IT...

1 Use a measuring cup to pour the same amount of water into each of the drinking glasses.

2 Add some salt to one of the glasses.

3 Use a plastic cup to pour some soil into the second glass.

4 Pour some fine sand into the third glass.

5 Stir all three glasses and leave them for a few minutes.

6 Compare the three glasses. You will see that the salt has disappeared. Most of the soil lies on the bottom of the glass. The water with sand in it is cloudy, with a layer of sand at the bottom.

WHY IT WORKS

Salt grains fall apart until they are so small that they can move unseen among the water molecules. They have dissolved. Sand and soil are both made up of small and large particles. Most of the soil particles are too big to dissolve and they sink to the bottom. The fine sand particles are small enough to be carried in the water in a cloudy mixture called a suspension.

SALT

SOIL

SAND

SEPARATING SUBSTANCES

WHAT YOU
NEED
Drinking glasses
Soil
Water
Sieve
Filter paper
Measuring cup

SOME SUBSTANCES DISSOLVE IN WATER better than others. But how easy is it to separate different substances from the water again? The project on this page will show you how to filter a mixture of soil and water. This will separate the mixture to give you what you started with: soil particles and clear water.

WHY IT WORKS

The holes in the sieve are small enough to stop some soil particles passing through, leaving the mixture a little clearer. The holes in the filter paper are even smaller and only let the tiniest particles pass through with the water. As a result, the mixture is very clear after passing through the filter paper several times.

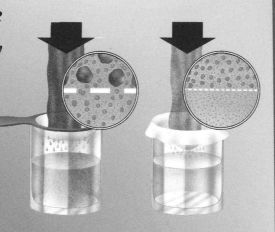

FILTERING

1 Pour water into a measuring cup and stir in some soil.

SOIL BLOCKAGE

Repeat the project without the sieve. You may find that the large particles block the holes so that no water can pass through.

2 Place the sieve over a glass and pour through the soil and water mixture. You will see that the water appears slightly clearer, while the sieve now contains particles of soil.

3 Make a cone out of filter paper. Place it over another glass. Pour through what is left of the mixture from the first glass. It will become even clearer and you will see tiny soil particles left on the filter paper.

4 Repeat with clean filter paper and a clean glass. Be careful not to remove the filter paper too soon, as the mixture may take time to pass through.

5 Repeat the filtering until the water running into the glass is clear. You have now separated the soil from the water.

BOILING APART

THE LAST PROJECT SHOWED YOU how to separate soil from water. However, not all substances are as easy to separate from each other. To separate dissolved substances, called solutions, more complicated methods are needed. These methods often make use of differences between the two substances. This project shows you how to separate a solution of salt and water by adding heat.

BRINGING TO A BOIL

1 Dissolve the salt in the water in a drinking glass.

2 Pour the solution into a saucepan. Ask an adult to boil the solution on a stove. It is very important that you ask an adult to do this for you.

3 When all the water has boiled away, ask an adult to turn off the stove and put the saucepan to one side to cool.

WHY IT WORKS

As the solution is heated, the tiny molecules in it shake rapidly as the heat gives them more and more energy. The water molecules eventually have enough energy to be able to fly off as a gas called steam. This is called boiling. However, the heat does not supply enough energy for the salt molecules to boil, and they are left behind.

WATER MOLECULES FLY OFF AS STEAM

4 Look into the saucepan and you will see a layer of white salt. Do not touch it, as it will still be hot.

SUNNY SAUCER

Leave the solution in a saucer on a sunny window ledge. The water will disappear, leaving the salt behind. This works in the same way as boiling the solution, but is slower.

ADDING HEAT

SOME FORM OF ENERGY IS OFTEN needed for a chemical reaction to start. The heat in a room may be enough for a substance or mixture to start changing, but in many cases, more heat is needed. For example, china plates and cups have been baked in a very hot oven called a kiln. This turns them from soft clay into hard china. This project shows how heat can turn flour and water into a hard substance

WHAT YOU NEED
Flour
Water
Large bowl
Skewer
Cotton thread
Paint

COOKING JEWELRY

1 *Mix flour and water together in the large bowl to make a dough. Knead the dough well to squeeze out any air bubbles.*

2 *Shape and roll the dough into beads like these. Sprinkle flour on your work surface to stop the dough from sticking. Ask an adult to make a small hole in each bead with a skewer. This will let you thread the beads when they are baked.*

3 *With the help of an adult, cook the beads in an oven until they have baked hard. Allow them to cool, then push the thread through them to form a necklace.*

4 *Decorate the necklace with the paint.*

MAKING IT EASIER

Change the dough ingredients by adding a little oil. This makes it easier to mold into shape.

WHY IT WORKS

When flour is mixed with water it forms a paste or a dough, where the flour molecules are suspended in the liquid. The consistency of the dough depends on how much flour you add. When the dough is baked in the oven, the heat causes the water molecules to evaporate (1), leaving behind a hard substance (2).

(1)

(2)

5 Wear the necklace yourself or give it to someone as a present.

ACIDS AND ALKALIS

WHAT YOU NEED
*Red cabbage
Kitchen knife
Jars, Saucepan
Water, Lemon
Blotting paper
Vinegar, Milk
Washing soda
Paintbrush*

ONE WAY OF DESCRIBING CHEMICALS is to say whether they are acids or alkalis. Acids, such as lemon juice, tend to have a sour taste, while alkalis, such as milk, tend to be slightly soapy to the touch. Pure water is neither acid nor alkali — it is described as neutral. Don't try tasting or touching chemicals at home, though. This project shows you a simpler and safer way to test whether a liquid is an acid or an alkali.

FOOD INDICATORS

You can make indicators from other fruits and vegetables. Blackberries and blueberries make good indicators and so do beets. Use these to test other liquids around the house.

DETECTING ACIDS

1 *Ask an adult to cut the cabbage into small pieces. Put it in the saucepan and cover it with water.*

2 *Ask an adult to heat the saucepan on the stove. Boil the water and let it simmer for 10 minutes. Remove it from the heat and let it stand for one hour.*

3 *Drain off the cabbage juice. Dip the blotting paper into it and leave it to dry. This will be your indicator paper.*

4 *Squeeze the juice from the lemon. Pour it, the milk, the vinegar, and the washing soda into separate jars.*

6 Use the other liquids to add different colors to your picture. Make sure that you rinse the brush after using each liquid. You will see that each liquid changes the color of the paper.

5 Dip the paintbrush into the lemon juice and start painting a picture on the soaked blotting paper.

WHY IT WORKS

The juice from the cabbage is a good indicator of how acidic or alkaline a substance is. The substance reacts with the liquid and changes color according to whether the liquid is acid or alkali. If the liquid is an acid, the paper will turn red or pink. If the liquid is an alkali, the paper will turn blue or green.

← ACIDS — NEUTRAL — ALKALIS →

209

BUBBLING VOLCANO

IN THE LAST PROJECT, you looked at differences between acids such as vinegar and alkalis such as milk. But what would happen if you were to mix acids and alkalis together? Farmers do this regularly, by adding alkali lime to acidic soil to make the soil neutral. This project shows what happens when you mix acidic vinegar with alkaline baking powder — the effects are spectacular.

CHEMICAL VOLCANO

1 Form the cardboard into a cone and wrap it around the plastic cup. Glue this firmly to a cardboard base.

2 Cut off the top of the cone, then glue newspaper strips onto it. Glue on five or six layers of strips. When the strips are dry, paint your volcano and let it dry.

3 Mix three parts of water with one part of glue and paint the volcano with the mixture. This will protect the cone when the volcano erupts. Let this dry.

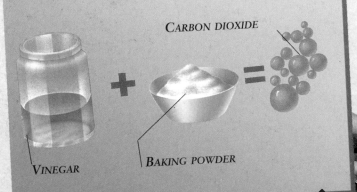

WHY IT WORKS

When the acidic vinegar and the alkaline baking powder mix they cause a reaction that releases bubbles of a gas called carbon dioxide. These bubbles of gas cause the mixture to foam up and erupt out of your volcano.

CARBON DIOXIDE

VINEGAR + BAKING POWDER =

4 Mix some red food coloring with the vinegar. Put a teaspoon of baking powder into the volcano.

5 Now pour in the vinegar and food coloring mixture.

FIZZY LEMONADE

Bubbles of carbon dioxide are what make fizzy drinks fizzy. To make fizzy lemonade, mix the juice of four lemons with water and some sugar. Stir in a little baking soda. Watch it fizz, and then drink it!

6 Watch as red foam erupts out of the volcano, like red-hot lava from a real volcano. The more chemicals you use, the bigger the eruption will be.

GIVING OFF GAS

WHAT YOU NEED
Cork
Used
matchsticks
Small candle
Tall jar
Long spoon
Splint
Baking powder
Vinegar, Water

WHEN A FIRE BURNS, a chemical reaction takes place between the burning substance and a gas in the air called oxygen. If there were no oxygen, the fire could not burn. To put out fires, firefighters spray water, foam, or even carbon dioxide gas to prevent more oxygen from reaching the fire. This project shows how carbon dioxide can extinguish (put out) a lit candle.

FIRE EXTINGUISHER

1 *Make a boat by pushing four used matchsticks into each side of a cork as shown. Make a hole in the cork and stick the candle into it. Float your boat in some water at the bottom of a tall jar. Ask an adult to light the candle using a splint.*

DIFFERENT SHAPES

See what different kinds of fire extinguisher you can find. Never touch a fire extinguisher as you are looking at it, as it might go off.

2 *Carefully add several spoonfuls of the baking powder to the water. Stir the mixture gently with a long spoon.*

3 Quickly pour some of the vinegar in the jar, making sure that you don't spill any onto the lit candle. The liquid should begin to fizz. If it does not, add more baking powder and vinegar.

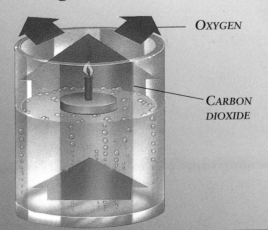

4 Watch as the liquids at the bottom of the jar fizz and bubble. The candle will dim and finally go out.

WHY IT WORKS

Mixing the vinegar and baking powder together creates bubbles of carbon dioxide. As these bubbles rise from the liquid, they push out the air that was in the jar. Without oxygen in the air, the candle can no longer burn, so it goes out.

OXYGEN

CARBON DIOXIDE

213

MAKING BREAD

WHAT YOU NEED
Dried yeast
Fine granulated
sugar
Warm water
Flour, Butter
Board
Oil, Salt
Large bowl
Plastic wrap
Baking pan
Damp dish towel

ALL OF THE REACTIONS YOU HAVE SEEN involve nonliving chemicals. These are called inorganic reactions. There are other types of chemical reactions involving living organisms. These are called organic reactions. This project shows you how bread is made and how the chemical reactions of a tiny mold called yeast make bread dough rise.

GETTING A RISE

1 Mix two tablespoons of dried yeast with one teaspoon of sugar and a cup of warm (not hot) water. Leave this mixture until it starts to foam.

WHY IT WORKS

The yeast mold contains chemicals called enzymes. These react with the sugar to release bubbles of carbon dioxide. The warm water speeds up this reaction. The bubbles of gas cause the bread to rise and take shape.

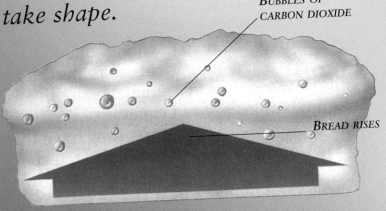

BUBBLES OF CARBON DIOXIDE

BREAD RISES

2 Mix five cups of flour, two tablespoons of sugar, four teaspoons of salt, and 1 ounce of butter in a large bowl. Add the yeast mixture and stir in some warm water to form the dough.

3 Place the dough mixture on a floured board and knead it for a while.

4 Rinse, dry, and lightly oil the bowl and place the dough in this. Cover the bowl with plastic wrap and leave it in a warm place for a few hours.

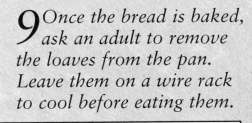

5 During this time, the dough will rise. When it has finished rising, take the dough out of the bowl and knead it again until it becomes firm. Mold the dough into loaf shapes.

6 Place the dough loaves on a lightly oiled baking pan, brush them with salty water, sprinkle with a little flour, cover with plastic wrap, and leave them to rise again.

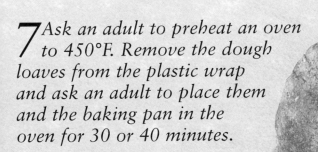

7 Ask an adult to preheat an oven to 450°F. Remove the dough loaves from the plastic wrap and ask an adult to place them and the baking pan in the oven for 30 or 40 minutes.

8 To check if each loaf is baked, ask an adult to use a damp dish towel to lift it from the pan and tap the base. If it sounds hollow then the bread is ready. If not, leave it in the oven a little longer.

9 Once the bread is baked, ask an adult to remove the loaves from the pan. Leave them on a wire rack to cool before eating them.

UNLEAVENED BREAD

Try making the bread without adding the yeast mixture. You'll see that the dough does not rise, and you will be left with what is known as unleavened bread.

SCIENCE WORDS

ACCELERATION This is the rate at which an object moves faster and faster.

ACID This is a type of substance that usually has a sour taste. Vinegar and lemon juice are both acids.

AIRFOIL A special shape that is designed to rise when air flows over and under it. A wing is an airfoil.

ALKALI This is a type of substance that is usually soapy to the touch. Baking powder and milk are alkalis.

AMPLITUDE The volume of a sound is known as its amplitude.

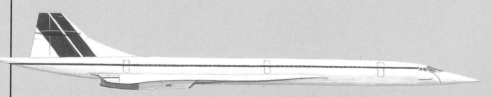

ARCH This is a natural or artificial structure that crosses an open area in a curve.

AREA This is the amount of space that an object covers.

AXLE This is a bar that connects a number of wheels.

BAROMETER A device that measures changes in air pressure and is used to predict the weather.

BOILING The process of turning a liquid into a gas by raising its temperature. You can boil liquid water to turn it into steam.

CAPILLARY ACTION The movement of a liquid along very narrow tubes.

CENTER OF GRAVITY This is an invisible point on an object through which the weight of the object acts.

COCHLEA The cochlea is a tiny organ found inside each of your ears. Inside is a fluid that is vibrated by sound waves. These vibrations are turned into signals that are sent to the brain, where the sound is heard.

COMPASS A tool for showing direction, using a magnetic needle that turns freely to point to magnetic north.

COMPRESSIONAL FORCE This is a force that squeezes something.

CONDUCTOR A material that will allow electrons to flow through it. Examples include metals and carbon.

DENSITY The heaviness of a substance for a particular volume.

DISSOLVING Dissolving happens when two substances, such as salt and water, combine completely. When one substance dissolves in another, the result is called a solution.

DISTANCE How far it is between objects.

DOMAIN Any of the tiny magnetic regions of a magnet or magnetic metal.

DRAG Air resistance caused by disturbances in the flow of air over an object. This force slows down moving objects.

ECHOES These are sounds that have bounced off a hard surface and can be heard after the sound has been made.

ELASTIC When a material is elastic, it is capable of returning to its original shape after it has been pulled.

ELECTRIC CIRCUIT The path around which an electric current flows. It includes a source of electricity, such as a battery.

ELECTRODE When sending an electric current through a liquid, such as a salt solution, the electricity is carried into the liquid by two conductors called electrodes.

ELECTROMAGNET An iron or steel object surrounded by a coil of wire that acts like a magnet when a current flows through the wire.

ELECTRON One of the tiny particles that make up atoms. Electrons have a negative charge. Whether moving or static, electrons are what we call electricity.

FLYWHEEL A heavy wheel that stores energy as it spins. This means it can keep spinning for a long time.

FREEZING The process of turning a liquid into a solid by lowering its temperature.

FRESHWATER Water that has very few dissolved substances, such as salts and minerals.

FRICTION A force that is created when

two objects rub together. It slows down the movement of these objects as they pass each other.

GEARS These are objects which are used to transmit force (move force from one place to another). Gears can be wheels with teeth, flat bars with teeth, or even screws.

GRADIENT This is a stretch of ground that slopes up or down.

GRAVITY The attractive force between objects. The earth's gravity keeps us on the ground.

HYDRAULICS The technology of liquids.

HYDROMETER An instrument used to compare the densities of different liquids.

ICE The solid form of water. Water freezes and turns into ice when the temperature gets below 32°F (0°C).

INDUCTION COIL The electromagnetic field created by a changing current flowing through a wire coil will cause a current to flow in a second coil.

ION A charged particle in a fluid.

LEVER This is a simple machine, usually a solid bar, which is used to transmit a force around a pivot to a load.

LIFT An upward force that is caused by low air pressure above a surface.

LINES OF FORCE Imaginary lines within a magnetic field curving from the north pole to

the south pole of a magnet.

MAGNETIC FIELD The space around a magnet where it has magnetic influence. Magnetic objects in this magnetic field are pulled toward the magnet.

MELTING The process of turning a solid into a liquid by raising its temperature.

MOLECULE The smallest naturally occurring particle of a substance.

OPAQUE When no light can pass through an object, it is called opaque.

ORGANIC A reaction is organic when it involves living things.

PENDULUM This is a weight that swings on the end of a long string or pole.

PITCH Notes can be high or low. This depends upon how quickly the sound waves that make up the sound vibrate. How high or low a note is is called the pitch. (See also next entry.)

PITCH The movement of an aircraft when the nose either rises or falls.

PIVOT This is a point about which an object rotates (moves in a circle).

PLASTIC A material is plastic if it can be shaped when it is soft and then sets hard into its new shape.

POLES Areas on a magnet or the earth where the lines of force are closest together and the magnetic field is strongest.

PRESSURE A force caused by the weight of the atmosphere.

PULLEY This is a wheel around which a rope is pulled to transmit force. Pulleys working together can reduce the work level (the amount of effort you put in) needed to lift an object.

REFLECTION This occurs when light rays bounce off a shiny surface, such as a mirror.

REFRACTION This occurs when light rays are bent as they travel through an object.

ROLL The movement of an aircraft when one wing rises and the other falls.

RUDDER A special paddle usually found at the rear of a boat. It is used to steer the boat.

SALT WATER Water that contains a high level of salts and minerals. These give the water a salty taste.

SHADOW A dark area caused by an object blocking out light rays.

SKYSCRAPER A very tall building, usually found in large cities.

SOLENOID A coil of wire wrapped around a cylinder. When a current flows through the wire, it acts like a magnet. Solenoids are used in switches and relays.

SOLUTION This is a fluid where one substance has dissolved completely in another one.

SOUNDPROOF A room or object that does not let sound pass through it is said to be soundproof.

SOUND WAVES Sounds spread out from their source as waves, similar to ripples on a pond.

SPECTRUM Using a specially shaped

piece of glass called a prism, sunlight can be split up into a band of colors. This band of colors is called a spectrum.

SPEED This is the rate at which an object covers a distance in a particular period of time.

STATIC ELECTRICITY This is a type of electricity that forms on the surface of certain materials that are rubbed together.

STEAM The gas form of water. Water boils and turns into steam when it is heated to 212°F (100°C).

STREAMLINED A streamlined object has a shape which helps it move through the air easily.

SUBMERSIBLE A craft that can go underwater and rise again to the surface at will.

SUSPENSION A suspension is when the particles of one substance float inside another fluid substance.

SUSPENSION BRIDGE This uses long cables hung from towers at either end of the bridge to help it take the weight of objects crossing it.

TESSELLATE When shapes tessellate, they cover an area completely without overlapping or leaving any gaps. Hexagons are six-sided tessellating shapes.

TRANSLUCENT When only some light rays are able to pass through an object, the object is known as a translucent object.

TRANSPARENT Objects are called transparent when they let light pass through them freely. You can

see through them completely.

VOLTAGE This is the force that pushes electricity through a wire, in a similar way to the pressure of water in a pipe.

VOLUME The amount of space that an object takes up in three directions, called dimensions.

WARP THREADS These are threads that run up and down a material as it is being woven.

WATERWHEEL A wheel that is turned by flowing water. Today, water-wheels, or turbines, are used to produce electricity.

WEFT THREADS These are threads that run across a

material as it is being woven.

WINCH This is a wheel that is turned by hand. A winch can be used to drive a machine or to wind in a rope.

WIND TUNNEL A device that is used to find out how streamlined objects are. It uses trails of smoke to see how air moves over the object's surfaces and how much drag the object creates.

YAW This is the movement of an aircraft when it turns either to the left or the right.

INDEX

INDEX

INDEX